How To THINK LIKE A CODER

WITHOUT EVEN TRYING!

JIM CHRISTIAN

BATSFORD

First published in the United Kingdom in 2017 by
Batsford
43 Great Ormond Street
London WC1N 3HZ
An imprint of Pavilion Books Company Ltd

ISBN: 9781849944458

A CIP catalogue record for this book is available
from the British Library.

25 24 23 22 21 20 19 18 17
10 9 8 7 6 5 4 3 2 1

Reproduction by Rival Ltd, UK
Printed by Toppan Leefung Printing Ltd, China

This book can be ordered direct from the publisher at the website
www.pavilionbooks.com, or try your local bookshop.

Distributed in the United States and Canada by
Sterling Publishing Co. Inc., 1166 Avenue of the Americas,
17th Floor, New York, NY 10036

Contents

LEARN HOW TO THINK LIKE A CODER!

Learn How to Think Like a Coder!

Learning how to code is essential to the technology and educational literacy of the current and future generations. Computers are in use daily to help make life easier for us, and as they become more prevalent and connected, we must ensure that we have the tools and the know-how to make them work. Once we begin to understand this, we can then make progress through 'talking' to them with the aid of available **programming languages**. One of the most common things that stops people from learning how to code is being unsure where to start, or even being unaware of the possibilities. The number of pathways you could take towards learning how to code can also be overwhelming.

One thing that unifies all the past, current and (hopefully!) future coding languages is a set of core concepts. You will find that these core concepts have their roots in computer science, logic and mathematics – and that is what we aim to show you to help you 'think' like a coder, without having to touch a line of actual **code** first. It is impossible to predict accurately what kind of technologies and advancements you will find yourself working on in the next few years, let alone decade – so we hope that learning these core concepts will equip you with a toolkit for life, no matter what gets thrown your way.

Your journey towards learning how to think like a coder will help you establish critical-thinking skills, improve upon your organisation and help build your confidence when working with computers, so that you won't be fazed by coding terminology when you encounter it further down the road.

Along our path towards learning how to think like a coder, you won't require a dedicated computer or need any specific software to run on it – a set of dice, a deck of cards, perhaps even something as simple as a pencil and paper will do the trick!

You will learn a little bit about everything, from how computers work and think to specific computer-science concepts like loops, 'if statements', variables and more by exploring how we can draw comparisons between the coding and natural worlds. This is a guidebook to help you discover more about the incredible world of coding.

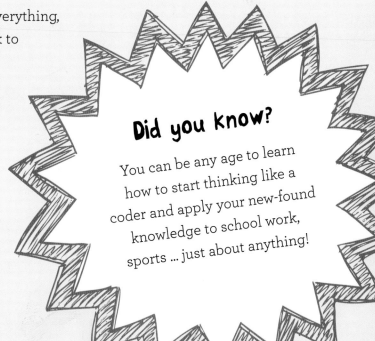

Did you know?

You can be any age to learn how to start thinking like a coder and apply your new-found knowledge to school work, sports ... just about anything!

What Is Coding?

What do you think of when you hear the word 'code'? Perhaps a secret code, in which words and letters are changed around to prevent messages from falling into the wrong hands, or used as a fun way to communicate with your friends without anyone else finding out what you're talking about? Well, you're not wrong! **Encoding** is the process of taking information and converting it into different forms, while **decoding** is the opposite – taking a coded message and turning it into a language that we can more easily understand.

Coding for computers is a lot like that too, as we convert our thoughts and processes into actions that we would like computers to do for us. We use programming languages to help us do that. Programming languages help bridge the gap between coders and computers by using words that we are more accustomed to understanding, and translating them into the language of numbers that computers can understand – binary. We'll learn more about binary later on (see page 20).

The most important thing to remember is that no matter how powerful computers are, the real power lies in the grey matter between your ears – your brain! Computer coders are the ones who help make computers do what they do, so let's get started and learn some more!

Did you know?

Even celebrities like the fashion model Karlie Kloss and musician will.i.am have learned to code to help express their own creativity!

Computers Are Everywhere

If you take a look around, you will find that computers are just about everywhere these days. We can see them in our homes, at work, at school and also when we are out and about! The most common place that we might find a computer, however, would probably be in our pockets in the form of a smartphone. In fact our pocket computers are more powerful than the computers that originally put astronauts on the moon nearly fifty years ago! Not to mention that they are much smaller, too. Computers used to take up entire rooms and were only able to do specific functions. Now they can be worn on our wrists and perform a multitude of tasks. Smartphones today can actually carry out tasks that we needed specific, expensive equipment to do only 25 years ago – imagine carrying around a phone, digital camera, video camera, computer monitor, calculator and more in your pocket!

Because computers are so accessible, we use them every day to help solve problems – and also entertain us. We might be so used to having computers everywhere that we don't even give it a second thought. Let's take a moment to consider the kind of computers we interact with on a regular basis.

EXAMPLES AT HOME

You might use:

- A smartphone to wake you up in the morning, make phone calls, take photos and play games.
- A wearable fitness computer to help track your health and fitness levels.
- A tablet computer to send emails, browse websites and use social media on the internet.
- A laptop or desktop computer to do some more specific tasks, such as editing video, creating music or playing games.
- A smart meter to measure your heat and power usage.
- A speech-activated device to order groceries, play music or perform an internet search.
- A toothbrush that displays how much time you should spend brushing.

EXAMPLES OUT AND ABOUT

Computers you might come across:

- When you check out your groceries at the store, a computer tallies up the cost, checks store inventory and takes payment from you.

- Automatic Teller Machines (ATMs) will check your bank balance and dispense money for you.
- Computers use facial recognition at passport controls to make travelling safer and more efficient.
- Crossing lights and traffic signals rely on a system of detectors and relays to respond to traffic changes and allow pedestrians to cross the road safely.
- Certain travel cards contain a chip that you swipe to use.
- Security systems can monitor areas with cameras and motion sensors.
- With an eReader (electronic book) you can read any book anywhere.

And so on. It's more and more likely that a greater number of items in your house might have computers and networking capabilities in them to help them talk, or do other things that you wouldn't normally expect them to do. How about a water filter that orders replacement filters automatically when it runs out? Or a light bulb that can change colour when given instructions from your smartphone? These are examples of a new trend called the **Internet of Things** (IoT), where single-purpose, everyday objects (such as a kettle or a doorbell) are made 'smarter' by putting a computer chip and network connectivity inside.

No matter their purpose, all these examples rely on computers and coders in order to operate correctly.

How Computers Work

Chances are good that if you have something in your house running on electricity or batteries, it also runs on computer code and has some (or all) of the features of a modern-day computer.

WHAT MAKES A COMPUTER A COMPUTER?

The outside of various computers may look very different. After all, we have phones, tablets, desktop and laptop computers, which all perform in different ways. But inside their cases they have a lot in common. Let's have a look inside a computer and see what goes on in there.

The Microprocessor

The microprocessor is the part of the computer that does the majority of the 'thinking'. It acts as the brain of the computer. A microprocessor may have more than one core on it, allowing it to follow even more instructions per second. The more cores a microprocessor has, the bigger its brain is, and the more instructions it can follow.

The microprocessor is also referred to as the central processing unit, or CPU. Within the microprocessor are hundreds upon thousands of switches, that are waiting for an electric signal. The electrical signals are then formed into pathways and gates that are either on or off, using a system called binary (see page 20).

RAM – Random Access Memory

This is the memory of the computer (usually measured in gigabytes). Just like human brains, computers can only remember a certain amount of information at a time. When a computer is performing a task, it takes up a percentage of available RAM until the task is complete. Since most computers will do more than one thing at a time, having plenty of RAM is a good thing.

Storage

A computer must also have somewhere to store all of its programs, and this is commonly done on a device called a hard drive. Storage is also measured in gigabytes. Having more storage on your own computer lets you keep more photos, movies and music files, for example. The internal storage on your computer is also called a hard drive. If you were to plug in a USB key to take some files with you, that would be called external storage.

Another term for computers being everywhere is **ubiquitous computing**.

Input and Output

A computer at home might have **peripherals** built in to it or attached to it, like a mouse and keyboard, webcam or printer. These are all means through which you can provide **input** to and receive **output** from the computer. For example:

- A webcam will take your picture and send it to someone else you're chatting with online. This is an example of the computer receiving input.
- A keyboard, trackpad and/or mouse will take input from your hands and allow you to give the computer instructions.
- The screen on your computer displays data, such as a webpage, a document you might be working on or the screen of a video game. In this case, the computer is providing you with output.
- Some newer devices, such as smartphones and tablets, allow you to touch the screen, making it both an input *and* output device.
- Additional input on most computers can be provided by plugging a device into a Universal Serial Bus (USB) port.

Network

Computers have a common means of talking to one another, whether it's wirelessly playing music on your headphones, or connecting to the internet to look up information on other computers all over the world. A computer might have a wireless connection (also known as Wi-Fi) which connects it to the internet router in your home or office. It might also have Bluetooth, another means of connecting devices such as wireless mice or headphones. Most desktop computers also have an Ethernet port for a physical, wired connection to a network.

Small-project computers such as the BBC micro:bit and the Raspberry Pi also have these parts, although the storage might be smaller – enough just to run one program – or, in the case of the Raspberry Pi, as large as the available memory card that you put into it.

These are only the basic parts of a computer. Other computers, such as our smartphones, also have light sensors that can automatically adjust the brightness of a screen, accelerometers to detect how fast the device is moving, gyroscopes to detect which way up the device is being held, compasses to aid with navigation and global positioning systems (GPS) to pinpoint your location. All these extra sensors allow the computer to do certain things when conditions on the computer change.

The majority of computers have these things in common: a brain to do all the thinking; memory to help it think; space to put things; and the ability to receive input and produce output.

The Motherboard

All of the aforementioned parts of the computer are connected through a larger board inside called the motherboard. The motherboard is where all the other components, or parts, of the computer are linked to one another so that electrical signals can be sent back and forth between them, transmitting and receiving information. Computers are not the only devices to have motherboards. They can be found in all other kinds of devices with electrical components that need to be linked together.

THE HUMAN COMPUTER

This is a lot like what humans and other animals can do. We have a brain, memory for thinking and storing, as well as the ability to receive input through our senses and output through our muscles. Not to mention, we all look different on the outside.

So would you say that there is much of a difference between humans and computers? If the microprocessor is our brain, then what is our input?

We can take input in through:

- What we see with our eyes.
- What we hear through our ears.
- What we smell through our nose.
- What we taste with our tongue.
- What we feel with our skin.

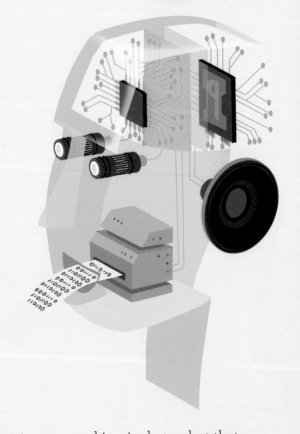

There are other ways we can sense input as well, such as knowing when we are off-balance and dizzy, feeling hungry or thirsty, or recognising that we are tired.

We have a large capacity for remembering things (but perhaps not all at once), and we also rely on external storage by keeping journals, taking photographs and even storing things on a computer.

We mentioned earlier that computer storage is measured in gigabytes, but that wasn't always the case. As storage has become cheaper over time, we tend to measure it in whatever the currently popular and most affordable capacity available is. At this moment in time, the gigabyte is the most common measurement of storage (you might have a 250GB hard drive with 16GB of RAM in your computer).

Here's a little more about storage:

Unit		Equivalent to...
Bit	0 or 1	Yes or No
Byte	A group of 8 bits	A typed character on your keyboard
Kilobyte (KB)	1,024 bytes	Two paragraphs of text
Megabyte (MB)	1,024 kilobytes	About a minute of digital music playback
Gigabyte (GB)	1,024 megabytes	Nearly 4,500 books (of average 200-page length)
Terabyte (TB)	1,024 gigabytes	Just over 230 DVD movies
Petabyte (PB)	1,024 terabytes	Just over 350 million photos

So by comparison, how much storage do we have in the human brain? It's been a topic of debate for many years now, with some neuroscientists thinking it's as high as 2.5PB, and others thinking it's as low as 1TB. We may never know the answer!

Did you know that the floppy diskette was once the most common external storage device. It was how computer users used to transport files before the internet and Wi-Fi became affordable and mainstream. That's why in most computer programs today, you'll still see an icon of the floppy diskette on the screen where you're meant to save your work.

How Computers Think

If our own brains have electrical impulses running through them to transmit information to other parts of the brain and body, how does a computer think? Again, it's strikingly similar.

BINARY

Binary is a way of counting, using only two numbers – 0 and 1. We control computers by telling small parts inside them (called **transistors**) to either be on or off so that electricity can go in the right directions and run a program. The 0 and 1 tell the transistors to either be on or off. Each 0 or 1 represents a bit (the smallest unit of computer storage).

All the input and output on a computer is represented by lots and lots of these binary numbers – whether it's your favourite video game, or a funny cat video on the internet. It's all made up of 0s and 1s being translated into code that your computer can understand. That kind of code is called **machine code**.

Did you know that the binary number system was developed by Gottfried Leibniz in 1679, over 300 years ago? In fact, evidence of binary systems has been found even further back than that.

A Brief Explanation of How Binary Works

One of the best ways to understand how binary works is to show you how to convert regular (decimal) numbers into it. With decimal numbers, we assign place values into columns, starting with the ones column, then the tens column, hundreds column and so on. Each column goes up by the power of ten as you move from right to left (this is also known as base 10, or a **denary** system):

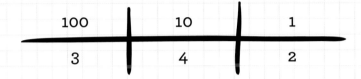

100	10	1
3	4	2

In the above table, we have a 2 in the ones column, a 4 in the tens column and a 3 in the hundreds column: three hundreds, four tens and two ones, which is 300 + 40 + 2 = 342.

Binary columns increase by the power of two as you move from right to left, like so:

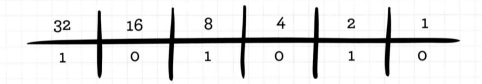

32	16	8	4	2	1
1	0	1	0	1	0

In the binary table above, there is a value of 1 in the 32, 8, and 2 columns, which we add up as 32 + 8 + 2 = 42. We would write that number as 101010.

All these 0s and 1s are the language that computers understand: on or off; yes or no; true or false.

Create Your Own Messages with Finger Binary!

To demonstrate how we can use what we know about binary already, here's a fun game that you can play to transmit messages to your friends using just your hands!

With both of your hands, you can only count up to ten. But if you use your fingers to represent binary numbers, you can count to 31 on just one hand! Here's how.

- Start with your closed fist; this will represent the number '0'
- Your thumb represents the number '1'
- Your index finger represents the number '2'
- Your middle finger represents the number '4'
- Your ring finger represents the number '8'
- Your pinky represents the number '16'

Knowing that there are 26 letters in the alphabet, you can assign each letter a binary value and represent that with your fingers. Use the table opposite to see what binary shape your hand needs to take to represent its corresponding letter.

What would the following message spell out? *

'1000 101 1100 1100 1111 10111 1111 10010 1100 100'

> There are 10 types of people in the world. Those who understand binary and those who don't!

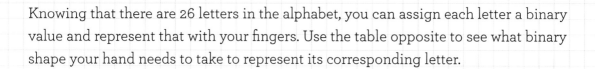

Extended Exercise

Of course, we can only count to 31 with just one hand using the finger binary method. But if we add our other hand, we can count all the way up to 1,023. Remember that each additional finger's value is twice the value of the finger before it. So if the pinky finger on our first hand has a value of 16, then the value of the thumb on the next hand is 32. The next index finger is 64, and so on.

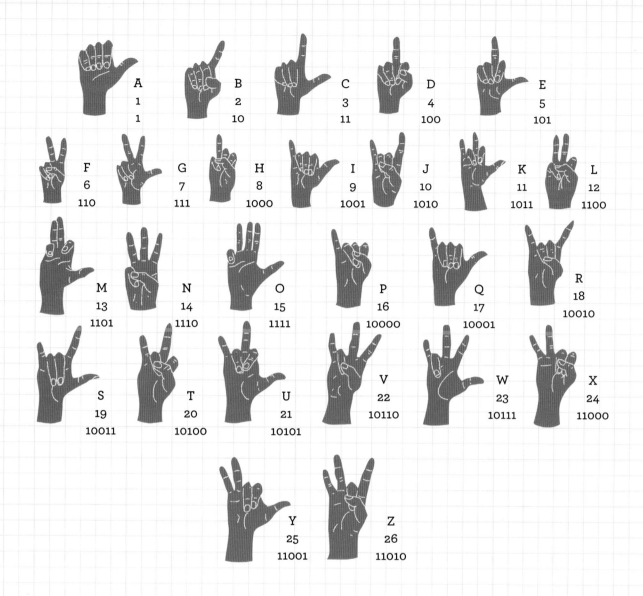

Letter	Number	Binary
A	1	1
B	2	10
C	3	11
D	4	100
E	5	101
F	6	110
G	7	111
H	8	1000
I	9	1001
J	10	1010
K	11	1011
L	12	1100
M	13	1101
N	14	1110
O	15	1111
P	16	10000
Q	17	10001
R	18	10010
S	19	10011
T	20	10100
U	21	10101
V	22	10110
W	23	10111
X	24	11000
Y	25	11001
Z	26	11010

Do you think that you could come up with your own trivia game where the answers are all numbers (no higher than 1,023 though!). What kind of questions could you ask? This would be a good game that exercises both the creative and logical hemispheres of your brain!

Binary is the number system that computers understand, but thankfully we don't need to know how to program in binary to get code working on a computer! There are modern programming languages that will take care of that for us, which we will look at later on. For now though, let's learn some more about the history of computers and coding to see how we got to where we are today.

* **Solution:** '1000 101 1100 1100 1111 10111 1111 10010 1100 100' spells out 'Hello World'! – one of the most common phrases and exercises used for those who are learning how to program.

Before Computers

What did we do before computers were a part of our everyday life, and how did we end up creating them to carry out tasks for us? It may be hard to imagine a world without computers these days – and to be fair, they've been around a lot longer than we might initially think, as we'll find out in the next chapter.

What makes a computer different from any other machine? Is your toaster a computer? Your bicycle? Maybe! A computer by loose definition is an electronic device that can take information, transform and store it, then output that information in a desired format. For example, a video games console takes information in through the controller, transforms finger movements into instructions for a game, then outputs that information through a screen that the player watches. Or a smartwatch might take your pulse through a sensor on the back, and output that information to a display on your wrist.

Computers, if not made for new reasons (such as the video-game example above) are usually introduced to replace older, non-working equipment that might have unreliable parts.

Take a traffic light, for instance. Older electro-mechanical traffic lights would have been made up of physical switches, gears, clocks and levers to work. Over time, the parts in that traffic light would start to wear down and need replacing, due to conditions like rust, friction and weather. To maintain and repair those traffic lights all the time cost money, so as soon as computer-controlled lights became cheap enough, it became **efficient** to install them instead.

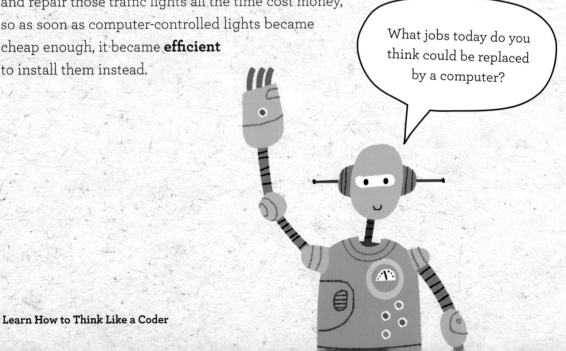

What jobs today do you think could be replaced by a computer?

Another example of how older systems have been modernised through the use of computers and networks is how we listen to music. About 30 years ago, if you wanted to listen to a music album while you were away from your stereo or car, you would buy a tape cassette (which held perhaps about an hour's worth of music) and put it into a portable music player – the famous Walkman. You could only put in one tape at a time, and to listen to the entire thing you would have to switch the tape to the other side (although more modern players would do this for you). Compare that to 15 years ago when the first portable music players started coming out boasting '1,000 songs in your pocket'! And today, internet access and mobile networks are cheap and reliable enough that we can **stream** as much music as we want to our devices without having to worry about running out of storage!

Getting a computer to replicate all those functions without having to rely on all those moving parts has over time become much cheaper to manufacture, install and maintain. So in many cases, code has taken over the role of mechanical jobs of the past.

Learning how to understand technology trends can help us predict how these changes will affect human and computer jobs in the future.

Coding and Computers Through History

Compared to the rest of human history, computers have not been around for very long. But you might be surprised to learn just how far back the history of coding goes. If binary has been around since the seventeenth century, how long have computers and coders been around for? Here is a brief timeline of notable events and people in computing history that have brought us to where we are today.

CHARLES BABBAGE (1791–1871)

Charles Babbage is widely considered to be the father of the digital programmable computer, even though he was never able to complete building one. Prior to calculators, people relied on other 'human calculators' to do mathematical calculating for them. These so-called human calculators would print out mathematical tables by hand, which were then copied into books. Babbage knew that because people could get tired and make mistakes, the tables were very prone to human errors. Given that the mathematical tables in question were needed for important fields such as navigation and the sciences, he also knew that this just wouldn't do. He devised a system through which the tables could be calculated through the use of a mechanical computer – that he called a Difference Engine.

A working model of Charles Babbage's Difference Engine was finally built and completed between 1991 and 2002 according to his original nineteenth-century plans and now resides in the London Science Museum!

ADA LOVELACE (1815-52)

Ada Lovelace met Charles Babbage during the proposed construction of his new device, the Analytical Engine. She was as enthralled with the possibility of his Difference Engine as much as he was impressed by her scientific and mathematical ability – he nicknamed her 'The Enchantress of Number(s)'. This new Analytical Engine was designed to take input through the means of **punch cards**, and was considered to be a programmable computer. In her notes of the time, Lovelace described an algorithm that would have used the Analytical Engine to calculate Bernoulli numbers (very important mathematical numbers that were sometimes difficult and time-consuming for humans to calculate), and for that she is credited as being the very first computer programmer.

ALAN TURING (1912-54)

Alan Turing is known for his work as a codebreaker at Bletchley Park during the Second World War, and for his contributions to the development of modern computer science. Turing also pioneered the field of **artificial intelligence**, and developed the **Turing Test**: a means through which humans can test if a computer is artificially intelligent enough to pass as a human. Recent examples of computers that have tried to pass the Turing Test are Deep Blue (the first computer to beat a human chess champion) and IBM's Watson (a computer that won $1,000,000 on the American game show *Jeopardy!*) His work has inspired others to continue pushing the frontiers of how computers can understand natural language and interact with humans (among other things).

SIR TIM BERNERS-LEE (1955-)

While the development of the internet can be credited to many working groups and individuals, Sir Tim Berners-Lee is hailed as the father of the World Wide Web (WWW). The WWW consists of web pages and hyperlinks (which we often just call 'links') that connect them together. Without his invention in 1989, we would most likely not have the ability to use the internet, search engines or many of the things that we have become accustomed to using.

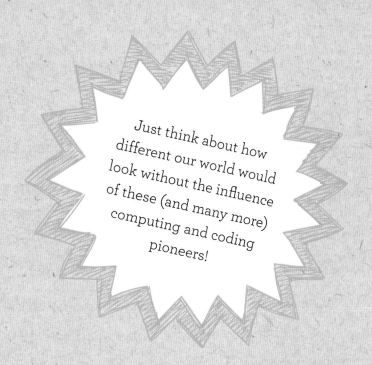

Just think about how different our world would look without the influence of these (and many more) computing and coding pioneers!

GORDON MOORE (1929–)

Gordon Moore made an observation in 1965 that the number of components that existed on a computer chip appeared to double every year, and would continue to double every year for the next ten years. Ten years later he updated his observation to say that the doubling would occur every two years. That statement became commonly known as 'Moore's Law', and became a standard that computer manufacturers attempt to hold themselves to: to shrink down the size of chips and be able to put more components on to them would possibly mean smaller, lighter and more powerful computers. Moore's Law has stayed more or less on target for the last half a century.

Absolutely Anybody Can Code

Whereas coding was once thought to be strictly the realm of the seasoned programmer, it has become easier and more affordable to code for everybody. Coding can be fun, expressive and creative all at the same time. It's a great way to come up with creative solutions to things and exercise your brain. You don't have to be afraid that it isn't for you – you can see from history that the very first people who learned how to code computers were those who simply needed to solve a problem. You can start at any age, whether it be nine years old or ninety.

Now, it is entirely possible that you might be thinking, what can I possibly make if I learn how to code? When would I ever need to do that? While it might be hard to visualise or to put into context what you might use coding for right now, you should try your best not to let that worry you. Once you begin to learn some of the ways coders see the world, the possibilities will become clearer.

WHAT CAN YOU DO WITH CODE?

Some jobs that will use the principles of coding have not even been invented yet, and it might very well be that you are the first person to create your own technology job of the future! You may be encouraged to get into coding to become the next Mark Zuckerberg, Bill Gates or Steve Wozniak. All of those people (and many more besides) created something with technology, and that technology has reached out

Did you know?

Another famous binary language is Morse Code – a method of transmitting text information by telegraph in the 19th century with dots and dashes.

If you're really stuck thinking about a reason why you should learn to code, have a think about a game or an app that you like, and consider how you might change it or make it better!

and affected the lives of people around the world. You may also wish to link your ability to code with humanitarian projects (see Coding for Change, page 119) – projects to help people who aren't that well off and need technological assistance. Being able to write your own code also gives you the flexible option of being able to work from almost anywhere in the world, as long as you have access to a computer and an internet connection.

THE WORLD NEEDS MORE CODERS

Having access to the internet is a wonderful facet of modern life, but it is important that we learn how to think critically and not rely on search engines to do the work for us. On your road to coding, you may be tempted to look online for solutions to problems that you stumble across. But be wary of implementing code (or any other information) from sources you don't know or completely understand.

We need more creators, and more importantly we need those creators to be able to make their own tools. Not to mention the tremendous sense of accomplishment you will get when you create something for other people. Coding is for everybody, and you can find ways to apply it anywhere – whether you're an artist, an executive, a cricket player or a scientist.

SOLVING PROBLEMS

Solving Problems

Learning how to think like a coder does not mean that you need to have a lot of special skills. However, having a desire to solve problems will certainly help! Chances are you already solve problems all the time – you just don't even realise it yet.

Think back to the last time you may have got lost and couldn't find your way to a new place. In hindsight, although it may not have seemed like a large problem, it's still a problem you were probably able to solve. You could have used a smartphone to navigate your way, called a friend for help, looked at a local map or even asked a passer-by to assist you. Just the simple act of getting help from another source is a demonstration of how we can solve problems.

Solving problems can be challenging, and on a regular basis it may also be a little tiring, but that isn't necessarily a bad thing for your brain. We need stimuli to make our brains think a little bit harder every day. Even if you aren't used to solving problems on a daily basis, you only need to start with smaller problems before you can tackle some bigger ones.

Regular brain exercises and problem solving can increase your ability to concentrate, your memory and your reflexes. So the benefits aren't just related to coding computers or thinking like a programmer – they are great for everyone.

How the Brain Works

Your brain is composed of two hemispheres – the right side and the left side. The right hemisphere of the brain controls the left side of your body, and is also responsible for your imagination, awareness of art and creativity. The left hemisphere of your brain controls the right-hand side of your body and is responsible for logic, language and reasoning skills.

Both parts of your brain need to be nurtured to carry out tasks from day to day. We get this in the form of nutrition from the foods we eat, the amount of water we drink and also by getting a good amount of sleep each day.

Physical exercise is also good – we coders tend to sit down a lot, but too much sitting and bad posture can be our worst enemy. That's why it's important to take proper breaks, stretch, go outside and get some fresh air. Something as simple as a brisk walk may even lead you to thinking your way out of a problem.

You can also exercise and stimulate the individual hemispheres of your brain with some simple activities.

Left Brain	Right Brain
Puzzle solving	Creative writing
Meditation	
Keeping a journal	
Learning a new language	Sketching or drawing

Learning to code is great as it exercises both parts at the same time – it's what is called 'whole-brain thinking'.

Complex Problems

Some problems may appear complex when we see them for the first time. When that is the case, we break those problems down into more manageable chunks that are easier for us to understand. Take, for example, the universe.

From what we know and theorise so far, the universe is a huge, ever-expanding place that we may never completely understand. It is literally the largest thing that we know about. We also know that if we break it down into smaller parts – like galaxies, then solar systems, then stars and planets – we can start to understand how the smaller parts make up the larger whole.

It's not important that we understand things this big all at once, either, so don't get discouraged. Most complex things are only complex because they are underpinned by smaller, simpler systems.

We can apply the same thinking to the science of chemistry. In order for us to understand all the chemicals that make up the building blocks of life, scientists have had to break down all the chemical components and their various states into what we now call the periodic table of elements. This table gives us a smaller roadmap that we can use to understand chemistry much better.

Can you think of examples of other complex systems that have been broken down into smaller and more easily identifiable parts?

When faced with a problem, you can always break it down into three simpler steps:
1. Figure out what the problem might be.
2. Think of different ways around the problem.
3. Test out your different ways around the problem.

Mental Exercises

What are some examples of ways to get our brains thinking? Just imagine what would happen if you attempted to run a marathon without any training! Similarly, you don't jump headlong into solving problems without doing any kind of warm-up. There are many ways of warming up your brain before you start coding or problem-solving. Doing the daily quick crossword in your newspaper, or trying out easy Sudoku, for instance, are suitable work-outs. From there, you could move on to some recreational mathematics or logic puzzles that use the power of deduction to solve problems (see pages 40–42).

Sudoku

Sudoku is arguably one of the most popular puzzles of recent times, and chances are strong that you can find it in any daily newspaper (or online, or in an app). A Sudoku game is a 9×9 grid where each row and column must contain the numbers 1–9. At the same time, the 9×9 grid is divided further into 3×3 subgrids that must contain the numbers 1–9 as well. At no point can the subgrids contain the same number twice, nor can the columns or rows. Each classic Sudoku puzzle begins with some of the numbers already in place to guide the player.
Puzzles with a higher difficulty have fewer starting numbers.

You can generate your own Sudoku puzzles just like the one opposite with an online generator: http://www.opensky.ca/sudo

A Sudoku puzzle might look like this:

6	8	2		1				
								8
	4			8	3	6		7
	1	4	3					
8			9		6			1
			4			7	9	
5		3	1	6			8	
2								
			7			2	1	6

Solution:

The correctly completed puzzle looks like this:

6	8	2	7	1	4	3	5	9
7	3	5	6	2	9	1	4	8
1	4	9	5	8	3	6	2	7
9	1	4	2	3	7	8	6	5
8	2	7	9	5	6	4	3	1
3	5	6	8	4	1	7	9	2
5	7	3	1	6	2	9	8	4
2	6	1	4	9	8	5	7	3
4	9	8	3	7	5	2	1	6

Three Brothers

Trying out logic puzzles can be another way of using both sides of your brain. See if you can solve this example from the renowned logician and mathematician (not to mention magician!) Raymond Smullyan (1919–2017). You happen to know three brothers – identical triplets whose names are John, James and William. John and James always lie, whereas William always tells the truth. A while back you lent John a considerable sum of money and he has yet to pay you back. One day, while walking down the street, you run into one of the brothers. If it is John, you are keen to confront him about getting your money back, but you aren't able to tell whether it is John, James or William. Using only three words, what question could you ask the brother to determine whether or not he is John?

Solution:

The correct question to ask is: 'Are you James?'. John is the *only* brother who could answer 'Yes':

	John (lies)	James (lies)	William
Are you John?	No	Yes	No
Are you James?	Yes	No	No
Are you William?	Yes	Yes	Yes

More Logical Statements

The famed writer, logician and mathematician Charles Lutwidge Dodgson (1832–98) is credited with introducing the first logic puzzles to help people strengthen their reasoning skills. In **syllogistic** puzzles of this kind, we are given two or more assumed premises (statements that, for the purposes of the puzzle, are true) and must draw a conclusion from them. The most common example of a syllogistic puzzle is the following:

- All men are mortal
- Socrates is a man
- Therefore, Socrates is mortal

Here is an example of one of Dodgson's puzzles, which is a little more entertaining to say the least!

- All babies are illogical
- No one is despised who can manage a crocodile
- Illogical persons are despised
- Therefore, babies cannot manage crocodiles

Can you work out the deduction to another of Dodgson's syllogisms?

- No one takes *The Times*, unless he is well educated
- No hedgehogs can read
- Those who cannot read are not well educated

Solution:

The correct deduction is: No hedgehog takes *The Times*.

OTHER MIND GAMES

Here's one last puzzle to get you thinking, by Martin Gardner (1914–2010). Gardner was another mathematician and magician (and was also something of an authority on Charles Lutwidge Dodgson) who was famed for his logic and mathematical puzzles. This last one is a little bit sneaky...

Write down the following letters on a piece of paper (or print them out):

NAISNIENLGELTETWEORRSD

Once you've done that, cross out nine letters so that the remaining letters spell a single word.

> Charles Lutwidge Dodgson may be well known for writing silly logic puzzles, but he was certainly more famous by his pen name: Lewis Carroll – the author of *Alice in Wonderland*.

Solution:

~~NAISNIENLGELTETWEORRSD~~

~~NINELETTERS~~

You might notice that the *amount* of letters we actually crossed out was 11.

But combined they spell 'nine letters', leaving the remaining letters to spell:

A S I N G L E W O R D

Brainteasers, word problems, in fact any games that make you think are a good way to get warmed up for coding!

Working with Constraints

You may have noticed from the puzzle examples earlier that you were limited by a certain number of **constraints**. Constraints are limitations (or rules) by which the game must be played. For instance, in our Sudoku example, three of the constraints are that the same sequence of numbers from 1–9 must not appear twice in any of the columns, rows or 3×3 subgrids. In this case, the constraints are part of the actual game rules.

In our logic puzzle, you are limited to only three words to deduce which brother you are speaking to. This particular constraint is designed to force you to think more efficiently – in other words, to produce the most effective solution using the fewest amount of resources (words, in this case) available. This is a constraint that you may come across very frequently as you learn to code, as you may be physically limited by available memory on a computer and need your program to be as small as possible.

Other constraints outside of the coding world might be time pressures (needing to submit your homework by the end of the week), or interaction with others (needing to get your report done so that another team can work on it).

On your journey, make a note of constraints that you see being applied to things that you work on, and don't be afraid to impose some upon yourself. It may someday make the difference between never getting your project off of the ground, and shipping something that you can fix and amend later.

THE RIVER-CROSSING PUZZLE

One of the oldest logic puzzles around is the river-crossing puzzle. It dates back to the ninth century and one later version of it goes something like this:

A farmer, a dinosaur, a goblin and a box of gold are all on one side of a river. The farmer has to get them all across in a boat, but the boat can only hold the farmer and one other thing (the dinosaur, the goblin or the box of gold). The farmer can't leave the dinosaur alone with the goblin (the dinosaur will eat the goblin) and the goblin can't be left alone with the gold (the goblin will eat the gold). How can you get them all across without losing the gold, goblin or dinosaur? Have a think about the answer and we'll come back to the problem in a moment.

What you may find unfair about this puzzle is that you are constrained by your inability to deploy a really creative answer. Why doesn't the dinosaur just swim across with everyone on his back? Why doesn't the farmer buy a bigger boat with the box of gold?

When coding, you will often find constraints. Some of those may be the computers that you're coding (perhaps there isn't enough hard-drive space, or perhaps your program takes up too much memory and the system only has a small amount to spare?). Or perhaps the constraint is time. Your coding project might be due in two days so you only have about a day's worth of coding left and not enough time to include everything. At times like this you might feel frustrated, which is understandable. It's up to you to find a way around your problem and come up with an optimal solution.

Solution

Let's get back to the river-crossing puzzle. Do you think you might have solved it? Here is the solution.

- The farmer takes the goblin across the river, leaving the dinosaur alone with the box of gold.
- The farmer returns to the dinosaur and the gold on the other side of the river, and takes the dinosaur across.
- The farmer takes the goblin back on his second return trip, leaves the goblin and takes the gold over to join the dinosaur on the other shore.
- The farmer then goes back again for the goblin before joining the dinosaur and the gold on the opposite side of the river.

You might have thought that the original constraints of this puzzle were just that you could not leave certain members of your party alone together. But you soon might have realised that there was one *lack of* constraint – and it was one that you weren't even told about! You weren't told that you could cross back over the river again as many times as you wanted and bring back members of your party you'd already taken to the other side.

The lesson here is that when you're problem-solving, keep a keen eye out for things that aren't there or for information that you haven't been given, as sometimes the answer lies in what cannot be seen. And what's more, expect the unexpected!

Keeping it Simple

Computers really aren't very smart. Using all the chips within them they may possess the brainpower to carry out many tasks very quickly, but it really is the coder or programmer that provides all the essential intelligence. Therefore, you have to be extremely specific when you ask computers to carry out tasks for you.

Some programming languages will already have some built-in commands ready for you to utilise. These pre-programmed libraries are what we call **functions**. We will come back to these later, but depending on the coding language of your choice, you can make a few general assumptions:

- The computer can accept input and provide output. This might be as simple as accepting keyboard and mouse movements, and outputting results to a screen, storage device or printer.
- The computer can recognise and process **data**, meaning that it can distinguish the difference between numbers, text and other data types.
- The computer can carry out mathematical tasks (after all, a computer relies completely on mathematics to work correctly) including handling **variables**, **logic** and **operators**.
- The computer can understand and plot directions, or coordinates on a map, for example.

Even with all that, we have to give the computer very specific instructions. So, you can't just tell it to make your bed, clean your room and fix you a sandwich – at least not until you've explained every single step required to carry those functions out. Let's look at an example.

CLEAN MY ROOM

To work out what steps it would take to clean your room, we have to define what a clean room looks like. What would you think the **success criteria** are for a clean room? Let's look at just three small things. If you decide to tidy your room, what are the top three things that you think need doing?

Well, if I had to guess, they might be:
1. The bed is made.
2. Dirty clothes are in the laundry basket.
3. Everything has been tidied away in cupboards.

Let's suppose instead of cleaning the room myself, I want to get a robot to do it. Luckily, I have KnowBot.

Me: OK. KnowBot, are you up for a task?
KnowBot: 1 (for yes)
Me: KnowBot, make the bed!
KnowBot: ... (just sits there).
Me: Ah, OK, KnowBot – this is how you make the bed.

1. You straighten the duvet.
2. You put the blanket neatly on top of the duvet.
3. You put the pillow on top of the duvet and blanket.

Me: Let's unmake the bed again. KnowBot,
now that we've shown you how to make the bed, can you have a go?

That's not *exactly* how it was done.

That's what we mean by being specific. Let's see if we can make the instructions easier to understand.

1. Spread the duvet evenly over the entire bed.
2. Tuck the bottom of the blanket into the bottom of the bed, then pull it up until it cannot go any further.
3. Finally, place the pillow on top of the duvet and blanket at the top of the bed.

It is also very important that the instructions for carrying out a task are done in the correct order.

As you think about how you want the end result of your programs to be, also think about how specific and ordered the steps need to be to get there. Let's go back and look at the conditions needed to tidy up my room. They were:

1. The bed is made.
2. Dirty clothes are in the laundry basket.
3. Everything has been tidied away in cupboards.

Because I took the time to define what the success criteria were for a made bed, KnowBot now has explicit instructions. I wonder what would happen now if I tell him to 'Make the bed'.

[KnowBot goes back over to the bed I've just made and looks confused.]
Me: Oh! Sorry, KnowBot! The bed is already made!

How do we stop KnowBot from making the bed if it is already made?

For now, we can do it with the help of a **flow diagram** (also referred to as a data flow diagram, or sometimes a flow chart). Flow diagrams are useful not just in computer programming, but in planning all kinds of complex things. It helps you to lay things out visually. A flow diagram is made up of different shapes and arrows:

- A **start/stop** is indicated by an oval.
- A **process** is indicated by a rectangle.
- A **decision** is indicated by a diamond.
- Arrows indicate how the symbols relate to one another.

Shown opposite is a flow diagram that KnowBot can follow to determine if he needs to make the bed or not. This is just a simple version of a flow diagram – there are many different variations used for business and also software development, and they can range from a simple one like this to a more complicated one.

Thinking like a coder often requires you to step away from the screen and use other tools to visualise what you want your program to do, and also share it with others.

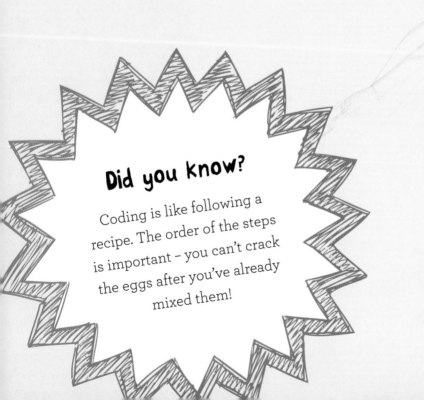

Did you know?

Coding is like following a recipe. The order of the steps is important – you can't crack the eggs after you've already mixed them!

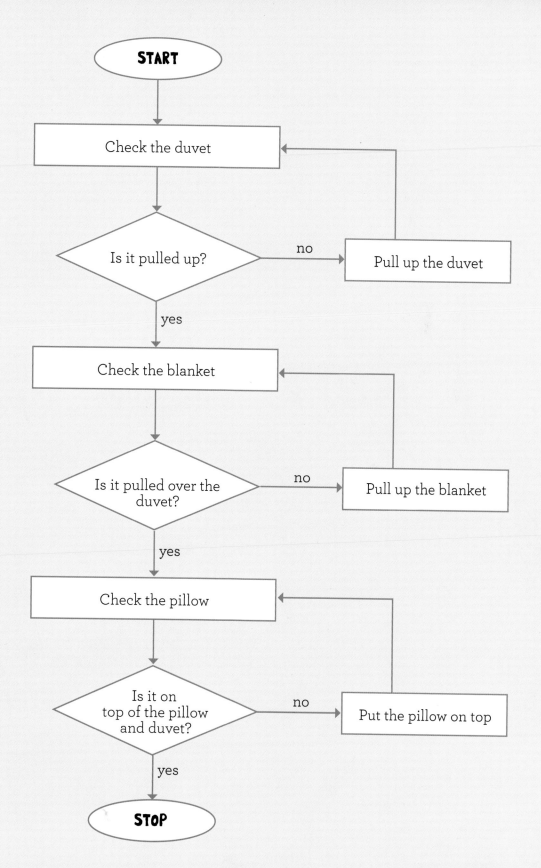

LEARNING THE LANGUAGE

Learning the Language

A programming language is the layer that sits between the coder and the computer doing what you want. Remember that a computer can only really understand binary (or machine code), which is represented by:

- 0 or 1.
- A yes or a no.
- An on or an off.
- A true or a false.

Machine code is made up of billions of tiny instructions designed to work on a specific computer's processor. And because not all processors are alike, machine code from computer to computer will be different. Trying to write machine code would be a daunting task, so we use programming languages to convert our intentions or actions into code that the computer will understand and **execute**.

Some programming languages are considered 'low-level' languages. You could say that they work at the lowest part of the computer, closest to the processor. Languages like this can be difficult to understand, and require that you know more about the physical computer you are running the program on. Other programming languages – 'high-level' – are designed to be easier to understand and write, but because they are so 'far away' from the processor, it can take more time to get that program ready to run. The current generation of computers is certainly fast enough that we don't really need to concern ourselves with that extra time, though, and high-level programming languages are what you will most likely encounter on your journey.

The following pages introduce concepts and terms that can be found in most programming languages. Remember that learning a new language (*any* new language) will often throw new rules and unfamiliar terms at you, so don't get discouraged!

Did you know?

If computer programming was a country, it would be amongst the most diverse on the planet, due to the number of languages spoken.

How You Say It

Syntax may be a term that you have come across before. It is not something that's specific to programming languages – it is found in *all* languages.

Syntax defines the rules around how we arrange letters, words, punctuation marks and phrases to make ourselves correctly understood. Consider the following two sentences:

'Let's eat, KnowBot!'
'Let's eat KnowBot!'

One missing comma can change the context of the sentence entirely! Sometimes accidentally adding or removing a character (such as the comma above) in your computer code can give you very unexpected results.

Whatever languages you speak and write with, you already know that the words have to be in a certain order and follow certain rules. The same is true with programming languages. When we speak and write, we do it with sentences. Each spoken and written language has its own rules for writing and speaking. When we translate 'Hello world' out of English, we already start to see changes to its structure.

In Irish:
Dia dhuit a domhan

In English:
Hello world

In French:
Bonjour le monde

When we write code, we do it with **statements**. A statement is the smallest piece of computer code that has an action attached to it. For instance, if we wanted to display the words 'Hello world' on a computer screen, there are different rules on how to do that:

In Java:
```
public class HelloWorld {
    public static void main(String[] args) {
        System.out.println("Hello world");
    }
}
```

In Python:
```
print("Hello world")
```

In Ruby:
```
puts 'Hello world'
```

You can already see that there are some key differences for one simple program between two modern programming languages. In Python, the addition and position of the parentheses () and quotation marks "" are crucial to the program working. In Ruby there is a minimum amount of special formatting required while in the Java example, the position of brackets and semicolons are critical. Additionally, both Python and Java require that the lines of code are correctly **indented**. Using the correct case (upper and lower) is also very important in coding syntax. These syntax rules are there to make sure that your instructions for the computer are written and understood correctly.

SYNTAX AND CONTEXT

Syntax plays an important role not only in how we write our computer code, but also in how we anticipate users interacting with it. A good example of this is the relatively recent rise of virtual assistants on mobile devices. This has drastically changed the way we can use technology, as we can now interact with them using natural language – our own voice.

Having a conversation with a virtual assistant is a unique experience of having to use syntax and also context. If you want to use the virtual assistant on your smartphone to see a film nearby, you might ask it something as simple as:

'Assistant, what movies are playing nearby?' and get accurate results back. You might also be able to use colloquial language: 'What's playing on the big screen tonight?' or 'Show me some films nearby,' and get similar results. Older, out-of-date language may not have the same effect: 'Please inform me as to the whereabouts of a moving-picture facility with programmes this evening.'

It is very clear that the coders behind these virtual assistants have tried to anticipate the many different ways in which their users will interact with them. Remember that thinking like a coder also includes thinking like the user of your code!

CHANGE A LETTER, CHANGE THE MEANING

Have a look at the list of statements below and see how adding or removing a letter or punctuation mark can completely change its meaning.

'Please exist through the gift shop.'
'Most of the time travellers worry about
    their luggage.'

Can you think of any others?

Answers

'Please exit through the gift shop.'
'Most of the time, travellers worry about their luggage.'

Remember that syntax isn't just about *what* you say, it's also about *how* you say it!

HELP FROM THE IDE

One tool that is of enormous help to a coder is the Integrated Development Environment, or IDE. This is the software tool that you will use when you write your code. Modern IDEs include **syntax highlighting**, which guides you as you write your code. Syntax highlighting changes the colour of the terms in your coding statements so that they can be more easily identified as functions, strings etc. (more on what those are later). Another feature of an IDE is autocomplete, which helps you finish your statements correctly. Some IDEs even have a referencing feature built in, like a library for the programming language you're working on, so that you can look up what terms mean as you code.

    Some IDEs are very simple text editors (like Atom), designed to work with many different languages. Other IDEs are specific: Greenfoot is designed for Java programming while XCode is designed for making apps for Apple computers. You will have many options to choose from, just like choosing the best tool for any job and you will have plenty of help on your journey to becoming a coder, even from your tools.

Forms of Coding

There have been well over a hundred different programming languages devised since the start of computer programming, but they certainly aren't all in use today! There are probably about ten to fifteen popular programming languages in use at any given time, depending on what you want to use them for.

Something else to consider with a programming language is whether you want to have an **interpreted language** or a **compiled language**.

With an interpreted language, a program that you create can be run on somebody else's computer without the need for them to do anything special. They would open the **file** you've created, run it and be able to interact with it as you originally intended. A common example of this is how we view pages on the World Wide Web. A web **server** serves out a particular webpage or game to hundreds of thousands of people across the world and they have the same experience, and can even play together (a good example of this is the popular web game *slither.io*) without having to install or download anything other than a web browser.

Compare this to a compiled language, where a program or app has to be packed into a single file (or an **executable**) that is specific to a particular device. You would not, for instance, be able to take your favourite app from your laptop and run it on your smartphone! You would need a differently compiled version of your program instead. New versions of these programs and apps need to be recompiled and installed every time – just like when you get updates on an app store, or a **patch** is released for one of your apps.

Another way to think about interpreted vs compiled languages is shown on the following pages.

LEMUR HOLIDAY

You have had a wonderful summer holiday abroad studying and drawing the lemurs of Madagascar. One particular lemur comes and sees you every day and waits for you to draw him in the same pose. Over a short period, you become the world's foremost expert at drawing the same lemur, and by the time you are ready to leave, Dante the lemur (as you have named him) packs his bag and decides to come back with you.

Upon your return, all of your friends, family and peers want one of your lemur drawings for themselves. So you decide to create a 'master' version of the drawing using your best paper and pencils, have it colour-photocopied at the best quality possible and distribute it among your family and friends. Everyone gets the same (interpreted) version.

Word soon gets around about how great you are at drawing your lemur and an editor from an art and nature magazine on the other side of the country calls up with an offer to feature your drawing in their next issue. They already have a copy of one of your master drawings, but it isn't in the right format to promote on their website. What's more, they need a scaled-up version for the humongous billboard outside their head office. After talking with the magazine about the technical specs of the art needed for the billboard, you text one of your art-school friends. She has a tablet that she uses for her drawings and agrees to let you borrow it to create a new 'digital' version of the lemur.

After you finish drawing it on her tablet, you export a version of the lemur at the largest size to fit on their billboard, medium size for their print magazine, and a small size for their website, and email it off to the editor. Three specifically compiled versions (and just one lemur)!

Other types of programming languages include **object-orientated languages**, **data languages** and **scripting languages**. If you are just about to get started with some of the common programming languages available (such as Python or Java), then you will be working with object-orientated programming.

Object-orientated Programming (OOP)

When you code with object-orientated languages, you will create objects. These aren't physical objects that you can hold and move around with your hands. They are virtual software objects that can do certain things and interact with other parts of your program. A good example of a physical object is you or me! And we can draw some similarities with a virtual object in object-orientated languages.

How would we create Dante the lemur with object-orientated programming? Let's start by looking at Dante's characteristics. He has black hair and orange eyes. He likes to climb trees, eat food and pose for drawings.

To think about that in terms of OOP, we start with a class of an object. A class is a blueprint that can be used over and over again. So if we wanted to create 'Dante' as an object, we would start with a lemur class. All objects made from our lemur class (or blueprint) will be exactly the same until we start to add some defining characteristics to them.

So let's create an object named Dante:

Object Class	Object Name	Object Properties
Lemur	Dante	Black hair
		Orange eyes

There are also things that Dante can do, which would be called actions (or methods):

Object	Method(s)
Dante	Climbs trees
	Eats food
	Poses for drawings

Now we have created a class, an object and properties and actions for that object. First off, Dante's hungry, so we had better create some food for him to eat. Let's begin by making a class called food:

Object Class	Object Name	Object Properties
Food	Lemur food	Made of insects and fruit

We put the new lemur food object in front of Dante and he tried to eat it, but for some reason it isn't working. No matter how hard he tried, he cannot eat the lemur food. Uh-oh! The problem is that we haven't given our lemur food a method yet.

Object	Method(s)
Lemur food	Can be eaten

Now that we've assigned a method to the lemur food (that it *can be eaten*), Dante can eat – what a relief!

For every object that you create, you also need to assign methods to it so that these objects can interact with one another. Just because we name an object 'car', for example, does not mean that it can be driven straight away.

Let's look at one more example. Dante likes to pose for drawings, so let's create some more objects that we can use to draw him. We'll start with a person class (and, just for this example, let's assume that all objects of a person class have arms, legs etc. and can do all of the things that a person can do). We'll also need to create some things to draw Dante with.

Class	Object	Properties	Methods
Person	You	Has hands	Can use pencil
		Has fingers	Can use sketchbook
			Can draw with pencil
Pencil	Drawing pencil	Black lead	Can be held
		Sharp	Can be used to draw
		Has eraser	Can be used by You
			Can be used to erase
			Can interact with sketchbook
Book	Sketchbook	Has paper	Can be used by You
			Can interact with pencil

Notice that when we created the pencil object, we specified that it was a *drawing* pencil. If you look in a stationery shop at all the pencils and pens, you'll notice that they all have different properties and uses – some have different colours, some have thicker points, some are better for writing and some are better for drawing. That's why we've created a specific 'drawing pencil' object of the pencil class.

When we created 'You' as an object we only included a couple of properties – that 'You' have hands and fingers. Granted, there are a lot more properties that make up you as a person! But when defining objects in OOP, we only put in the most relevant properties. Would it matter if the 'You' object had brown hair and was wearing a red T-shirt in this case? Would it make a difference to how 'You' worked with the pencil?

Think about some objects that you have lying around the house. If you have more than one television, for instance (say one upstairs and one downstairs), you might also have two remote controls called the upstairs remote and the downstairs remote. A property of both these remote controls would be that they take batteries. What kind of methods would they have? Can they change the channel? Can they increase the volume? Can they be used by anybody?

A quick-fix solution for a software program that has gone wrong is called a **software patch**. This term comes from the paper and punch-card era of programming computers. Code was physically cut out of a punch card, then replacement code was 'patched in'.

Different Types of Data

All the information that ends up going into a computer is made up of 1s and 0s, whether they are made up of pictures or text, numbers etc. But just as we can classify different species in the animal kingdom, we can also classify different kinds of data that we use in programming computers, and there's a very good reason for doing that – so that computers don't get confused and can do the right things with the information we give them.

Being able to identify and describe what kind of data we want to use helps the programming languages understand what it is that you eventually want to do with that data, how it can be stored, and what it represents. This is another example of computers not being able to understand what we mean unless we *explicitly* tell them.

If I told you I needed to go and put petrol in my tank, what would you picture? Or if I said that I needed to put away my cricket bat? Chances are that you would picture me filling up the petrol tank of my car and putting away a piece of sports equipment – not putting petrol into a large military vehicle and then stashing away a small flying mammal (who just so happens to play cricket!).

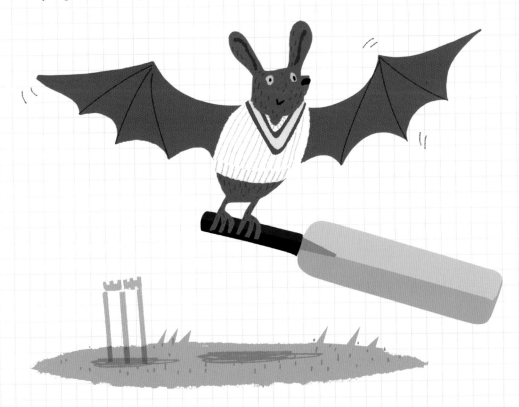

Just as a computer will not understand homonyms (words that sound and are spelled alike but with different meanings), neither can they tell the difference between the number 2 and the word two. For this reason, we use data types to categorise the different kinds of data that a computer can understand and manipulate.

So, what kinds of data types are there?

STRINGS (ALSO REFERRED TO AS TEXT)

Strings are an ordered sequence of characters. You may remember from earlier that characters are any symbol or letter that a computer can display. That includes letters, punctuation marks and numbers too. Strings can be short, as in only one word long, or they can be made up of many words like a sentence.

Example: The word 'string' is a string, and the sentence 'This is a string!' is also a string.

Strings can also contain numbers (remember, because numbers are a character, they can also be a string), which may be confusing until you start coding. There is a very good reason for this, though. Think of an example where you would want a number to be a string (so that you would not want to perform any calculations on it). What about your phone number or your postcode? It's highly unlikely that you would want to add any of those together, so the correct format to put them in would be as text. Not to mention that, in many places, phone numbers begin with the number 0, which would be removed from the phone number if it were stored as a number data type.

NUMBERS

You may already know that there is more than one particular kind of number, and that also applies to coding. First off, we have integers. **Integers** are whole numbers, such as the numbers 0 through to 10. An example of an integer is someone's age (e.g. she is 12 years old). They can have a positive or a negative value, but cannot contain any decimals. That's where real or floating point numbers – numbers such as 0.5, 7.2 and 10.315 – come in. **Floating point numbers** can have positive and negative values. Examples of real (floating point) numbers are latitude and longitude coordinates (such as 4.815 162.342) or temperature (37.5°C).

BOOLEAN

A Boolean, like binary, only has two states: true or false. Remember, binary is a counting system using 1s and 0s that can only be in two states: off or on. But we can equally explain it with any kind of opposite, such as up and down, negative and positive or in and out. A Boolean data type is used to answer questions where there are only two possible answers, yes or no.

DATE AND TIME

Date/time data types store date and time values! This might seem like a simple data type, but different countries display their dates differently.

If we take the date 21 October 2015 as an example, in the United States of America it would commonly be displayed as 10/21/2015 (month/day/year), whereas in the United Kingdom it would be displayed as 21/10/2015 (day/month/year). We use data types like date/time to make sure everybody is talking about the same date!

Choosing and using the correct data type can also determine what format that data gets displayed in. For instance, you would not be able to put in the date 42/13/5446 (at least, not on this planet!).

BLOBS

A BLOB stands for **B**inary **L**arge **OB**ject, and represents a large multimedia file, such as an image, music or video file.

Some programming and data languages may categorise data types into even smaller versions. For example, SQL (a Structured Query Language designed for accessing and utilising databases) has a DATE data type for year, month and day values, a TIME data type for hour, minute and second values and a TIMESTAMP data type that stores year, month, day, hour, minute and second values.

Data Structure

We have different data types, but sometimes we will need to find a way to sort through that data and ensure that it is organised so we can use it more efficiently. When we looked at 'Finger Binary', each hand gesture was matched up to a number, which was then matched to a letter in the alphabet (see pages 22–23). Without that structure, we wouldn't have known what all the finger binary signs meant.

Algorithms

Algorithms may have an unfamiliar name and sound complicated, but really, an algorithm is just a clear set of actions to be taken in a given order to achieve a certain task. We explored algorithms briefly back in Keeping it Simple, when KnowBot was given a clear set of instructions in order to make the bed (see pages 46–51).

The more specific the instructions are in our algorithms, the more accurate it can be, and the less prone to error when it is run. Remember that algorithms are just recipes for computers to follow. Let's try to give KnowBot instructions on how to make a cheese sandwich:

1. Pick up a slice of bread.
2. Put it on the counter.
3. Take the lid off the butter.
4. Set the lid down.
5. Pick up a butter knife by its handle.
6. Hold the butter knife with the handle in your hand and the blade facing away from you.
7. Lower the knife and drag it along the butter for three seconds.
8. Raise the knife.
9. Move the knife near the bread.
10. Lower the knife and drag it along the bread for three seconds, twice.

We're already ten steps in and have only just finished buttering one side of the bread!

11. Put the knife down on the counter.
12. Pick up a slice of cheese.
13. Put the slice of cheese on to the buttered bread.
14. Pick up another slice of bread.
15. Place it on top of the slice of bread with the cheese on it.

Notice how specific the instructions are, right down to how to hold the knife? It's possible that we could have been even more specific, even stating the angle of the knife and the speed at which it did the buttering. Speaking of which, you will also see that in steps 7 and 10 we did something interesting, which was to tell the computer how long to butter for. After all, KnowBot won't be able to tell when it has enough butter on the knife, and when the bread has been thoroughly buttered. So we have had to estimate that it might take about three seconds to do each.

STEP THROUGH

There is an old adage that goes: 'Measure twice, cut once'. In essence, this means that it is more efficient to double-check than to go back and correct! This should become an unwritten rule for you as you begin to think like a coder. You can check your algorithms by *stepping through* each step and seeing that it makes sense.

Let's look at another example of an algorithm, using a game designed to guess a person's age, with the help of some mathematics.

GUESS THE AGE

In this 'mathemagical' trick, you can convince your friends that you can guess their age without them even telling you. Here's how it works.

1. Your friend writes down her age on a piece of paper
2. She doubles it
3. She adds 1
4. She multiplies the result by 5
5. She adds 5
6. She multiplies that result by 10
7. She takes away 100
8. She crosses out the last two digits of the result

The number that she is left with is her age, in just eight simple steps.

If you're ever unsure of how many steps it might take to accomplish a task, try doing a simple chore in the dark – you may find that you concentrate more on the details!

Basic Loops

Up to this point, we've had to do a lot of work – especially when it comes to writing out algorithms. If programming languages are meant to be so helpful, surely there's a way they could stop us having to write repetitive instructions?

Thankfully, there is – with loops. Loops are designed to help us be more efficient by allowing us to repeat instructions. You've most certainly encountered loops before. The biggest loop that you're a part of every year is the Earth going around the sun! It repeats every 365 days. A smaller loop than that? How about the Earth making one complete turn every 24 hours? Loops are everywhere you see events repeating themselves.

Let's use a loop to simplify some basic instruction. If I was standing 10 paces away from you and I wanted you to come to me, I might say:

'Take 1 step towards me.'
'Take 1 step towards me.'
'Take 1 step towards me.'
'Take 1 step towards me.'
'Take 1 step towards me.'
'Take 1 step towards me.'
'Take 1 step towards me.'
'Take 1 step towards me.'
'Take 1 step towards me.'
'Take 1 step towards me.'

By the end of it, I would be exhausted from having to give you so many instructions, and you would probably be extremely irritated at being told to do the same thing ten times in a row.

It's also possible, had I given you written instructions, that I might have typed an extra number by accident and told you to 'Take 13 step towards me,' (which, while grammatically incorrect, you might do anyway)!

You may have already guessed that a better solution would be for me to ask you to:

'Take ten steps towards me.'

... which uses a loop! Loops are designed to repeat instructions a set number of times until a process has been completed. There are two kinds of loops: those that are controlled by numbers (or counting) and those that are controlled by conditions (which we'll look at in more detail on pages 81–87).

FOR LOOPS

A loop that is controlled by numbers is called a 'for loop'. For loops will repeat instructions for a set number of times, no matter what the outcome is. For instance, there might have been a brick wall between you and me when I asked you to take your steps, but (if you were following my instructions to the letter), that wouldn't have stopped you from trying to take ten steps in my direction. You may have been stopped midway by the wall, but you still would have correctly carried out my instructions.

WHILE LOOPS

A loop that is controlled by certain conditions being met is called a 'while loop'. The loop will continue to run *while* waiting for the conditions to be met. If I told you to:

'Take a step towards me until you reach me.'

... then that would be different from my previous instructions of asking you to take only 10 steps towards me. It might take you a while to get through that brick wall, though!

If we look at the cheese sandwich from our previous algorithm, what would be an effective use of a loop there (remember that we only got around to buttering one slice of bread)?

Building a better cheese sandwich

1. Pick up a slice of bread.
2. Put it on the counter.
3. Take the lid off the butter.
4. Set the lid down.
5. Pick up a butter knife by its handle.
6. Hold the butter knife with the handle in your hand and the blade facing away from you.
7. Lower the knife and drag it along the butter for three seconds.
8. Raise the knife.
9. Move the knife near the bread.
10. Lower the knife and drag it along the bread for three seconds, twice.
11. Repeat steps 1–10.

Notice that just by adding one more instruction, we can save ourselves some time (and potentially make a better-tasting sandwich). Now that we have amended the first part of our algorithm, is there anything we need to do to the rest of it?

12. Put the knife down on the counter.
13. Pick up a slice of cheese.
14. Put the slice of cheese on to one of the buttered slices of bread.
15. Pick up the other buttered slice of bread.
16. Place it on top of the slice of bread with the cheese on it.

We've had to amend one step in our algorithm to account for the already buttered slice of bread. By introducing a loop into our algorithm, we were able to do (nearly) twice the programming with one additional statement.

Some of you may have realised that by adding that loop into our algorithm, we've created a new problem. We never actually told our cheese sandwich-making program to stop repeating steps 1–10! Remember, computer programs are designed to do exactly as you tell them. Step 11 creates an infinite loop – something that should be avoided. The way our algorithm is written now, the computer will continue to butter new slices of bread until it cannot find any more bread to butter and eventually crashes. That's not good and we need to fix it! We can do that by amending step 11 to read:

11. Repeats steps 1–10 until two pieces of bread have been buttered.

We've given our algorithm a specific condition to fulfil before it can finish the loop. Now we can enjoy a tasty (and efficiently made!) cheese sandwich.

MORE LOOPS

In the instructions for this popular card game, can you spot the loops?

Go Fish Rules

Players: 2–6
Objective: To collect as many 'books' of cards as possible. A book is made up of any four of a kind (such as four aces, four twos etc.)

1. Deal five cards to each player (if only two to three players are playing, deal seven) then put the remaining cards face down in the middle to form the 'pond'.
2. Starting from the left of the dealer, the first player can ask any other opponent for a card that is the same rank as one of their own cards. They cannot ask (or 'fish') for a card if there is not a matching one in their hand.
3. If the opponent has any of the requested cards, they must hand them over to the player.
4. The player then continues, asking other opponents for matching cards.
5. If the opponent does not have a card they have been asked for, they tell the player to 'Go fish'. The player then has to take a card from the pool in the middle. It is now the next player's turn.
6. Once a player has a set of four cards of the same rank (a book), it is removed from their hand and placed in front of them.
7. If a player has no cards left, they have to take one from the pool and add it to their hand.
8. When the cards in the pool have run out, the game is over. The player with the most books of cards wins.

As early as step 1, we can see our first loop where the dealer gives cards out to each player (loop 1). You can imagine how tedious it would be if the instructions were: 'Give a card to the first player. Now give a card to the second player,' etc. With just one instruction, the dealer can either deal a minimum of 14 or a maximum of 30 cards.

Then, in step 2, we see the start of another loop, where the game begins (loop 2). The player then asks for cards until no more cards can be had from opponents (loop 3). Loop 1 is eventually closed when the game has finished and a winner is declared.

An example of when we hear loops all the time is when we listen to music. The next time you are listening to something, can you identify which part of the song repeats again and again? What about different instruments?

Conditional Statements

Conditional statements (also referred to as conditions) are simple ways for a computer to make a decision based on the information it has been given. We saw this in our loops. You already work with conditions every single day, whenever you make a decision. Think about how certain weather conditions may affect your choices regarding appropriate clothing. For example:

> *If* it is raining outside,
>> *Then* I need to take my umbrella.
>
> *If* the crossing light is green,
>> *Then* I can safely cross the street.
>
> *If* my phone has finished charging,
>> *Then* I can unplug it.

Conditional statements generally start with 'if'. As in: 'if *this* event happens, then do *that* thing'. We can add further options and specificity to our conditional statements with the use of **else**. For example:

> *If* it is raining outside,
>> *Then* I need to take my umbrella.
>
> *Else*
>> I will just wear a jacket.

> *If* the crossing light is green,
>> *Then* I can safely cross the street.
>
> *Else*
>> I might get hurt.

> *If* my phone has not finished charging,
>> *Then* I should leave it plugged in.
>
> *Else*
>> I will not have a full battery when I go out.

If you remember, back in Keeping it Simple we already learned how to do this with our flow diagram, helping KnowBot make the bed (see page 51).

In our original flow diagram, KnowBot would check to see if certain conditions had been met in order for him to make the bed. If they had not, he would complete the step and move on to the next one. We can express the steps KnowBot took as conditional statements:

> **If** the duvet is not pulled up,
>> **Then** pull up the duvet.
> **Else**
>> Move to the next step.

> **If** the pillow is not on top of the duvet,
>> **Then** put the pillow on top of the duvet.
> **Else**
>> Stop.

We can simplify this even further by assigning Boolean values to the state of the duvet, blanket and pillow.

> **If** duvet pulled up = TRUE,
>> Proceed to next step.
> **Else** if duvet pulled up = FALSE,
>> Pull up duvet.

> **If** pillow on top = TRUE,
>> Proceed to next step.
> **Else** if pillow on top = FALSE,
>> Put pillow on top.
>> Stop.

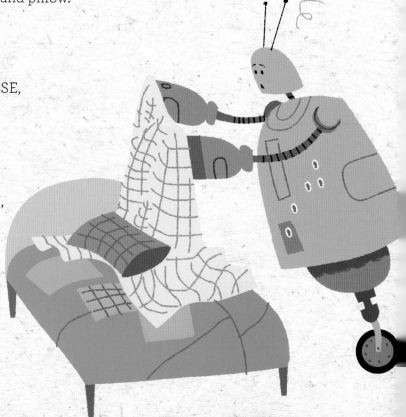

In this last version of KnowBot's bed-making algorithm, we are starting to evaluate conditions based on whether things are true or false. 'Duvet pulled up' = FALSE is the same as saying 'Duvet pulled down' = TRUE, and the algorithm we have written takes into account for both true and false values on the duvet, blanket and pillow. However, we want KnowBot to take action whenever one of our conditions evaluates as false (we want him to take action when the bed *isn't* made, not when it *is*). There is another, and simpler, way we could consider expressing this, with the algorithm below:

> **If** duvet pulled up = FALSE,
>> Pull up duvet.
>
> **Else**
>> Proceed to next step.

> **If** blanket pulled up = FALSE,
>> Pull up blanket.
>
> **Else**
>> Proceed to next step.

> **If** pillow on top = FALSE,
>> Put pillow on top.
>
> **Else**
>> Stop.

Both of the last two algorithms are essentially correct, but which one do you think might be more efficient? While they both have eight lines, could you say that one of them is more efficient than the other? Keep in mind that being efficient is not just about having fewer steps – it is more about making sure the steps themselves are as meaningful as possible.

In our second example, we don't need to put in an extra condition 'if duvet pulled up = TRUE'. We've already taken care of that by saying: If the duvet isn't pulled up, pull it up. If it is, move along. The *Else* is taking care of the TRUE for us.

As the old adage goes, it's quality, not quantity!

MORE CONDITIONAL FISHING

Let's take another look at the game of Go Fish. If you go back and look at the rules, you can see that there are some conditionals in there as well! They aren't always hard to spot: conditionals usually start with the word 'If'. Can you spot them all?

Go Fish Rules (with Conditionals)

1. Deal five cards to each player (if only two to three players are playing, deal seven) then put the remaining cards face down in the middle to form the 'pond'.

   As soon as we reach the first game rule we also see our first conditional statement:

   If the amount of players is less than or equal to three, and greater than one.
   Then deal each player seven cards.

Now we move to the second rule:

2. Starting from the left of the dealer, the first player can ask any other opponent for a card that is the same rank as one of their own cards. They cannot ask (or 'fish') for a card if there is not a matching one in their hand.

   Another conditional here in step 2:

   If the player does not have a card of a specific rank.
   Then the player cannot ask for a card of that rank.

3. If the opponent has any of the requested cards, they must hand them over to the player.

This conditional in step 3 is practically already written for us! Could it be worded any differently?

4. The player then continues, asking other opponents for matching cards.

5. If the opponent does not have a card they have been asked for, they tell the player to 'Go fish'. The player then has to take a card from the pool in the middle. It is now the next player's turn.

In step 5 the conditional has three actions that depend on it.

If opponent requested card = FALSE,
Then opponent tells player 'Go fish'.
      Player takes card from pool.
      End turn.

6. Once a player has a set of four cards of the same rank (a book), it is removed from their hand and placed in front of them.

Here in step 6, is a conditional that does not contain the word 'if'!

If player has book,
Then remove book from hand.

7. If a player has no cards left, they have to take one from the pool and add it to their hand.

Another one with clear conditional instructions:

If player cards == 0
Then remove card from pool.
        Add card to hand.

8. When the cards in the pool have run out, the game is over. The player with the most books of cards wins.

Even with conditionals, we have to be specific, as illustrated by this joke: John is about to go out to the grocery store and asks his wife if they need anything. She tells him: 'Please pick up a loaf of bread. If they have eggs, get a dozen.' John comes home with 12 loaves of bread!

Our last game rule and conditional statements:

> **If** pool cards == 0
> **Then** game over.
> **If** player books are greater than opponent books,
> **Then** player wins.
> **Else** *if* opponent books are greater than player books,
> **Then** opponent wins.

Notice that the statement 'The player with the most books of cards wins' actually requires us to specify what happens to the winner and also the loser of the game.

Go Fish is a simple card game, with easy to follow rules and gameplay – it just goes to show that you can think like a coder about anything!

Smooth Operators

You might have noticed that a couple more things were introduced to you while we were looking for conditionals in a card game, and those would be evaluation (or comparison) operators. You might be wondering why some of the equals signs were doubled up – it wasn't a typing error.

We use conditionals to evaluate for true and false, so using operators is just a way of giving us more chances to do that. Here is a list of some comparison operators and what they do:

Operator	Description	Example	Returns
==	Equal to	1+1 == 2	true
!=	Not equal to	2 != 2	false
>	Greater than	10 > 5	true
<	Less than	10 < 5	false
>=	Greater than or equal to	6 >= 4	true
<=	Less than or equal to	(5-1) <= 4	true

We use a single equals sign (=) in other places when coding to assign other values and meaning to things called variables, which we will look at later on (see page 98).

LOGICAL OPERATORS

Conditional operators weren't the only thing snuck into the last example. We can also control the flow of conditionals with logical operators. You'll remember that we touched on logic when we looked at mental exercises to warm up your brain (page 38).

Here's how logical operators work:

Operator	Description	Example	Returns
&&	And	(1+2) && (4-1) == 3	True (one plus two and four minus one are both equal to three)
||	Or	(2 == 3) || (2 == 1)	False (two is not equal to three and neither is two equal to one)
!	Not	!(3==2)	True (three is not equal to two)

With the knowledge of these new conditional and logical operators, how can we make the first instruction:

> **If** the amount of players is **less than or equal** to three, **and greater than** one,
> **Then** deal each player seven cards.

...even simpler?

Solution:
If amount of players <= 3 && > 1
Then deal each player seven cards.

The Psychic Penny

In this magic trick, we can use conditionals to determine which penny someone has picked up and held. You'll need five copper pennies, a table, and a friend to play the trick on.

The setup:
Lay the five pennies out on the table. Tell your friend, 'I have a mystical way with money. I don't speak about it often as it only seems to work with small denominations, but as you are such as good friend, I don't mind showing you this small wonder.'
Or words to that effect. If your friend agrees, tell them, 'Look at the five pennies on the table. Please feel free to examine any of them, or move them around.' Your friend does so. 'Now,' you tell your friend, 'I am going to turn my back. Please take a penny of your choice and hold it up against your forehead.'

As your friend picks up a penny from the table, tell them to push it hard against their forehead, and to think as hard as possible about the penny, as if they were transferring psychic data across the ether to you. Keep this up for about 30 seconds, then tell them to put the penny back on the table in the same position where it was taken from.

Once your friend has done so, tell them, 'Aha! Now the psychic information has been transferred! All I need to do now is wave my hands over the monies in question to determine which is the mentally linked coin!' As you wave your hand closely over the pennies on the table, you should be able to feel heat rising off the one that was attached to your friend's forehead for half a minute. You produce the coin to your friend's amazement.

Can you spot the conditional in this magic trick?

If the penny is warm,
Then that is the penny chosen by your friend.

You can find conditional statements in a lot of places, *if* you know how to look for them!

A logician's wife is having a baby. As soon as it is born, the doctor hands the newborn to the father. His wife asks: 'Is it a boy or a girl?' to which the logician replies: 'Yes.'

Fun with Functions!

Wouldn't it be great if you didn't have to code absolutely every part of a computer program and some of it was already done for you? Well, that's where functions come in.

A function is, simply, a block of already prepared and written code available to you in a programming language. The statements have already been put together ready for you to use – these are known as built-in functions.

Built-in functions can differ between programming languages, but they exist to stop you having to rewrite what has already been done.

Some examples might include being able to do basic or complicated maths, generate random numbers and print text to the screen. With functions, a lot of the hard work is already done for you so you don't have to spend time re-inventing ways to do things.

Here are three built-in functions from the Python programming language:

Function	What it does
int()	Converts a number or a string to an integer (it changes the data type)
print()	Outputs data to the screen
randint()	Generates a random number

In the Python examples above, we have two parentheses () with nothing inside them. Those parentheses are waiting for us to provide them with an argument. Now I don't know about you, but when I think about an argument, I think about two people having a heated discussion about varying opinions! But in the case of functions, the argument is there to provide the function with specific information that acts as input (these are independent variables – which we'll cover on pages 98–105). We saw the print() function before – when we learned about syntax, like this:

    print ("Hello world")

So we provide a function with an argument (input) to use with the function's output. In the case of our print() function with the 'Hello world' argument as input, the output on a computer screen would be:

Hello world

That sounds great, right? What's even better is that you can define your own functions as well – you don't have to rely solely on the built-in ones that come with the programming language of your choice. So if you have an algorithm that you would like to use more than once in your code, you can save it as a function and reuse it over and over again.

A CLOSER LOOK

A function is an activity that occurs naturally within something else. This definition doesn't just apply to computers. If we look at our bodies, it's easier to notice the regular functions that are 'pre-installed' on our human operating system. They are so automatic that we don't even notice they are there most of the time! When, for example, is the last time you checked that you were breathing?

Take a minute and notice your breath: inhaling and exhaling. Breathing a vital function of our body, as without it we wouldn't be able to get oxygen into our blood and pumped around to all the organs in our body.

If you were able to open up your brain and look at your built-in operating system, you might find two functions called breatheIn and breatheOut, running on an infinite loop – what might that look like?

Function	Actions
breatheIn (inhaling)	Contract diaphragm.
	Expand lungs.
	Draw in air from nose and mouth.
	Air travels down windpipe.
	Air enters air sacs in lungs.
	Oxygen from air moves into bloodstream.
breatheOut (exhaling)	Carbon dioxide moves from bloodstream into air sacs.
	Diaphragm relaxes.
	Air is pushed out of the lungs, through the windpipe and out of the nose and mouth.

These are 'pre-built' algorithms and loops built right into you!

An important point to note about built-in functions in programming languages is that they aren't always there until you need them. This is another example of efficiency – we only include what we need. If we included every single available function in all of our code, then our code would be very busy and bloated.

If I want to use some functions relating to time or maths, I would 'borrow' (or import) them from my programming language in my code. Then I could do all sorts of mathematical operations relating to time and maths in my code.

Now, the last time I checked, my lungs didn't know how to do maths (at least, I don't think they do!). But if I wanted to time how long it takes me to inhale and exhale or slow down my breathing, I would need maths to get the job done. In my human operating system, I would import my maths functions from another part of my body: my brain.

What other functions does our body have that run without us thinking about it?

The Magic 8 Ball

The Magic 8 ball is a handheld novelty toy from the 1950s that would pretend to tell the future. Floating inside the ball in blue-dyed liquid was a twenty-sided dice with different answers printed on to each face. Somebody using the Magic 8 Ball would ask it a simple yes or no question (like a Boolean), then turn it over and read the answer on the dice that floated to the top and could be read from a window on the back.

The answers that the Magic 8 Ball would have are as follows, structured into yes, maybe and no categories:

Yes	Maybe	No
1. It is certain.	11. Reply hazy, try again.	16. Don't count on it.
2. It is decidedly so.	12. Ask again later.	17. My reply is no.
3. Without a doubt.	13. Better not tell you now.	18. My sources say no.
4. You may rely on it.	14. Cannot predict now.	19. Outlook not so good.
5. Yes, definitely.	15. Concentrate and ask again.	20. Very doubtful.
6. As I see it, yes.		
7. Most likely.		
8. Outlook good.		
9. Yes.		
10. Signs point to yes.		

Out of the twenty possible answers, we have ten that are positive, five that are negative, and another five that are 'maybe' answers.

If we had to design a Magic 8 ball game using nothing but a pencil, paper and some dice, how could we do it? Where are our algorithms, loops, conditionals, variables and functions?

You may find in some programming languages that the terms 'function' and 'method' are used interchangeably. However, the definition can change depending on what language you use. Object-orientated languages (such as Java) define methods as something else entirely!

Magic (Paper) 8 Ball

For this game we would need either four five-sided dice or five four-sided dice to choose a number between 1 and 20. However, seeing as it's more likely that you have six-sided dice around the house, we can increase the available answers to 24 and only use four six-sided dice.

Yes	Maybe	No
1. It is certain.	11. Reply hazy, try again.	18. Don't count on it.
2. It is decidedly so.	12. Ask again later.	19. My reply is no.
3. Without a doubt.	13. Better not tell you now.	20. My sources say no.
4. You may rely on it.	14. Cannot predict now.	21. Outlook not so good.
5. Yes, definitely.	15. Concentrate and ask again.	22. Very doubtful.
6. As I see it, yes.	16. I'm not sure.	23. Are you kidding?
7. Most likely.	17. Yes. I mean no. Wait. What?	24. 100%, without a doubt, not going to happen.
8. Outlook good.		
9. Yes.		
10. Signs point to yes.		

This is for two or more players. One person acts as the '8 Ball', while the other players get to ask questions. One player asks a question, which has to have a 'yes' or 'no' answer. The '8 Ball' shakes four six-sided dice (or one die four times), adds the result together and references it on the answer table above.

The game requires us to generate a random number between 1 and 24 to enable us to look an answer up on the table. In this case, we're 'importing' a random number generator function from our dice, and they're taking care of the maths for us. Thanks, dice!

Can you spot the bug in the rules? If you only use a 6-sided dice, you will never get a number under 4. How can you adjust your answer table?

Variables

We mentioned variables briefly in the last chapter when describing functions (see page 92). A variable is like a container with a name and a value. We can put whatever kind of data we want into it, and we can also change the value of that data depending on how we want to use it.

Some of the most commonly seen uses of variables are in video games. A character's health or the amount of lives left are both variables. The *name* of the variable stays the same (e.g. 'Lives') but the *value* of the variable can change (e.g. the amount of player lives decreases when the character dies).

You can have variables too. When you were born, your eyes may have been a different colour than they are now, your height has increased and you have gone up in age:

Variable Name	Value
EyeColour	Green
Height	150cm
Age	16 years

You will always have these variables, and the values might remain the same after a while, or change depending on your physiology (most certainly you will age!).

Variables are, simply put, labelled boxes for things (you may also notice that variable names tend to not have any spaces in them).

SNOWMAN

A guessing game of Snowman is a great place to examine where variables occur. A game of Snowman is for two or more players.

Rules

The first person (PlayerOne) thinks of a secret word, and draws out blank spaces as placeholders for the letters of the word (for this example, let's use the word 'binary').

The second person (PlayerTwo) then guesses letters for the secret word. For each correct guess, the placeholder is filled with that letter. For each incorrect guess, the letter is written below the placeholders with a line through it. If there are more than two players, then a new player can have a guess if the player before them makes an incorrect guess. Play continues until the player attempts to guess the word and does so correctly, or until nine mistakes have been made and the players lose the game.

For every incorrect guess, a part of the snowman is built:

1. First incorrect guess: the lower (and largest) snowball at the bottom.
2. Second incorrect guess: the middle (medium-sized) snowball for his torso.
3. Third incorrect guess: the smallest snowball on the top (for the head).
4. Fourth and fifth incorrect guess: the snowman's left and right arms.
5. Sixth incorrect guess: a top hat on the snowman's head.
6. Seventh and eighth incorrect guess: each of the snowman's eyes.
7. Ninth and final incorrect guess: a carrot nose.

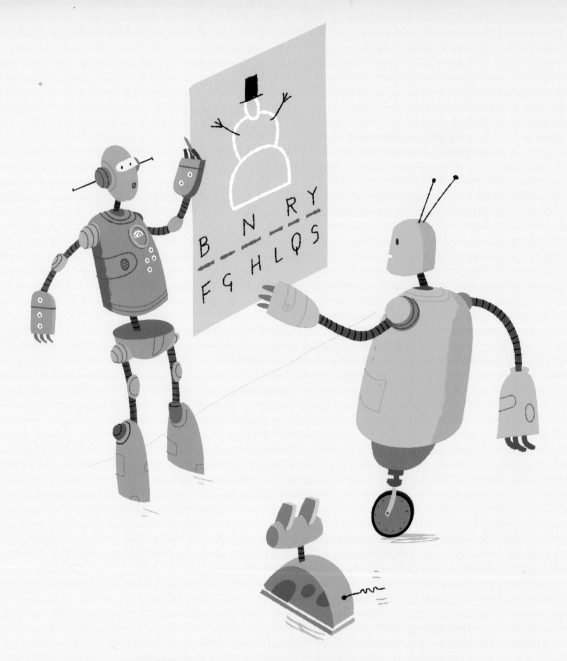

Where are our variables? In Snowman, the first variable we can identify is the mystery word (which we'll call MysteryWord). To PlayerTwo at the start of the game, MysteryWord could be any six-letter word in the dictionary. MysteryWord is a box with an unknown value to the player. To PlayerOne, who chose the value of MysteryWord, MysteryWord = 'binary'.

Another identifiable variable in this game would be the player's guess (PlayerWordGuess). PlayerOne knows that at any point during the game PlayerTwo will attempt to guess MysteryWord. PlayerOne can then evaluate whether PlayerWordGuess is equal to MysteryWord.

Let's say PlayerTwo asks: 'Is the word "brainy"?'

MysteryWord = 'binary'
PlayerWordGuess = 'brainy'
(MysteryWord == PlayerWordGuess) = FALSE

I'm afraid not, PlayerTwo, but you're welcome to try again!

Controlling Play with a For Loop

Remember when we said for loops are controlled by numbers? (see page 75). In turn-based games like Snowman where play is determined by the amount of turns a player has before the game ends, we can use a variable in our loop while it runs.

We know that it takes nine incorrect guesses for the game to be over for everyone. So we can create a variable called 'incorrect guesses' with a value of '9' at the beginning of each game: incorrect = 9.

We also want to subtract one incorrect guess away from the 'incorrect' variable every time a PlayerWordGuess is incorrect. So:

If PlayerWordGuess != MysteryWord
Then incorrect = incorrects – 1

If we remember our operators, != means 'not equal to'. So if the PlayerWordGuess isn't the same as the MysteryWord, then we subtract one from incorrects. Remember that we can add and subtract from the value of a variable without changing it, just as we can add and subtract to a player's score in a video game.

What happens when we run out of mistakes to make?

If incorrects == 0
Then stop.

Game over!

THE ANSWER IS THREE

Remember our age game from Algorithms on page 72? There is a similar one that you might have played before that uses a variable – and you probably haven't even realised it yet!

Variables change, depending on their required use. In the example below, a person supplies us with their age and we perform some mathematical operations on it.
No matter what number we are given as our input, the result will always be three.

1. Ask a person to think of a number.
2. Ask them to double it.
3. Ask them to add on 6.
4. Ask them to halve the number.
5. Ask them to remove the first number that they thought of.
6. Tell them that the result is 3.

You could change step 1 so that the person uses their age as the first number, so the variable here will be the person's age. I want my program to work on people of all ages, so the last thing I want to do is code it so that it only works on people of particular ages. I might call the variable personAge and we could write it like this:

$$((((personAge \times 2)+6)/2)-personAge) == 3$$

It might be tempting to name your variables funny things that don't seem relevant to your project (like wangDangDoodle or crumpetMonster). Keep in mind that you never know where your code might end up – so best to make sure that your variable names make sense to the widest range of people possible!

TEAKETTLE

In this Victorian parlour game, a player chooses a homophone (a word that sounds the same but has different spellings and meanings) and then creates a sentence using both meanings of that word – but instead of saying the actual word, the player says 'teakettle'.

For example: 'I heard that a thief tried to **teakettle** that **teakettle** girder from the building site.' (Answer: steal/steel)

The goal is to then try to discover what the mystery word is, while having a conversation with the player. The player must continue using the 'teakettle' variable in their replies, as demonstrated here:

Guesser: 'So, what did you do today?'
Player: 'I had to **teakettle** myself against the cold.'

The conversation continues until someone guesses the word and earns a point. If nobody is able to guess, then the player earns a point and gets to go again.

In this example, we actually have *two* values for our teakettle variable. So how is that possible? We do it with an array. An array is a variable with a group of possible values – it groups data items (of the same type) together under a single name. In this last round of the game, the variable 'teakettle' has the value of steal or steel. Either one of the two values can be substituted wherever the word 'teakettle' is uttered: teakettle = steal/steel.

I PACKED MY BAG

Another fun game that makes use of arrays is the car game I Packed My Bag. In this game, the first player begins by saying, 'I packed my bag and in it I put . . . my lemur.' The next player then says, 'I packed my bag and in it I put . . . my lemur and my sketchbook.' And so on.

Play continues until someone fumbles the order of the list, or forgets the list entirely. The last person who successfully 'packed their bag' is declared the winner.

In this instance, we're creating a variable array (let's call it packingList) and continually adding on to it until somebody 'runs out of memory' to store the variable array in their head any longer (hopefully they don't crash)!

MAGIC 8 BALL (REVISITED)

If we go back and look at the Magic 8 Ball from earlier (see page 96), we could also express the answers in the answer table as an array from 1 to 20 (or 0 to 19 – see below).

A note about arrays

When working with code and computers we count from the number zero instead of the number one. In the Magic 8 Ball game with paper and dice, we have to count from 1 as the dice (from which we're importing our 'random' maths function) do not have a 0 on them. If we were to translate this into a computer program with the table answers in an array, we would ask the computer to generate a random number between 0 and 23 (instead of 1 and 24).

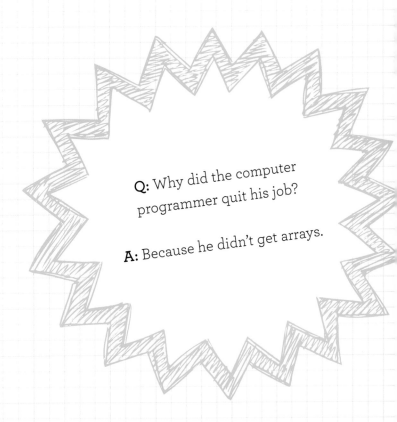

Q: Why did the computer programmer quit his job?

A: Because he didn't get arrays.

Debugging

One of the most important things you will learn when thinking like a coder and learning how to code is that not everything will always work the first time. This happens to absolutely everyone, so don't get disheartened. Computers can't think like we can, and (for better or for worse) they can only do what they have been told. To that end, you will probably find that you spend more time **debugging** your code than creating a solution from scratch with the programs you write (remember that we had to correct our cheese sandwich algorithm three times to get it to work). With each iteration of your program, though, you will probably discover new ways of doing things.

WHAT DOES DEBUGGING MEAN?

Although the term 'debugging' appears to have been around in other industries before its popular use in working with computers, it is attributed to US Admiral Grace Hopper who, while working on a Mark II computer at Harvard in the 1940s, discovered an actual bug (or moth in this case) that was stuck in one of the computer relays and stopping it from operating correctly. She is reported to have said that they were 'debugging the system' and the term stuck.

Just like many of the other terms we've explored so far, debugging isn't something that is specific to computers or computer science. In fact, Albert Einstein once used the term 'bugs' to describe 'little faults and difficulties' in the late nineteenth century. You might also hear the words 'glitch' or 'gremlin' used to describe the same symptoms of something unidentifiable (so far) getting into your systems and messing things up.

Debugging is what is know as going through your processes, your algorithms or flow diagrams and removing problems that are stopping them from working correctly.

KINDS OF BUGS

We can break bugs down into two different types – syntax and logic bugs. **Syntax bugs** are when we have made mistakes in how we've said or written something down. **Logic bugs** are when an error has been made in the way instructions are carried out and an algorithm has not gone according to plan.

See if you can spot the syntax bug in the following algorithm:

How to Pet a Cat

1. Pick up cat.
2. Put cat on your lap.
3. Pet ca.
4. Put cat down.

I'm missing a letter in step 3. If a robot or a computer was trying to run this program, they would keep looking for a 'ca' to pet until they eventually crashed.

How to Pet a Cat

1. Pick up cat.
2. Pet cat.
3. Put cat on your lap.
4. Put cat down.

Here we are able to pet the cat, although we haven't put it down yet. Surely picking it up, petting it, then putting it in our lap means we got the logical order of the algorithm wrong?

How about an example of a syntax *and* a logic bug?

How to Pet a Cat

1. Pick up cat.
2. Put cat on your lip.
3. Pet ca.
4. Put cat down.

That's right, I accidentally typed 'lip' instead of 'lap'. Even though the instructions were able to be followed and understood, they almost certainly had an unexpected outcome!

Going back through your code line-by-line can be a long and arduous task when looking for bugs. Fortunately, most programming languages IDEs can help you find problems before they even happen (most of the time, your programs won't even run until the IDE checks that they're OK).

In the event that you aren't running your code through an IDE, your first part of troubleshooting is looking for the specific part of your algorithm that isn't working. Say you've programmed a car game and the arrow keys on your keyboard that are meant to control the car aren't working. Where is the best place to start looking? What if you can't find where that bit of code is? Aha! That's why we comment our code wherever possible.

COMMENTING YOUR CODE

Because we haven't really been looking at actual code in this book, we haven't delved straight into how to put comments in – and different programming languages (of course) have different ways of adding comments. But let's take some of our pseudocode from previous chapters and look at how we could put in comments. Comments are written alongside your code. But, unlike your code, comments won't be recognised by the computer as something that needs to be run. That's because we put a special character in front of each line of commented code that tells the computer to ignore it.

```
# The line below will output Hello world to the screen
print("Hello world")
```

In the above Python example of 'Hello world', we just added one line above it starting with a # (you can say hash or hashtag if you want, but the real name of this character is an octothorp!). The # indicates to Python that anything else in that line should be ignored. You can put as many lines of comment in as you want:

```
# Hello World v1
# A. Coder
#
# This is my first Python program.
#
# The line below will output Hello world to the screen
print("Hello world")
# That's all – bye now!
```

The program is eight lines long, even though it only has one line of code! Use commenting wisely – remember that you may spend days and weeks writing a program and if you make comments and notes in your programs describing what you do, your future self will thank you for it.

```
# 23-Nov-2016 2203hrs
# A. Coder
# Added new code to evaluate playerGuess variable against
# mysteryWord variable
(mysteryWord == playerWordGuess) = FALSE
```

Keeping your code and algorithms (even if you're just planning on paper) well commented will save you a lot of time down the road when you end up having to troubleshoot. It also helps others if you work on coding projects collaboratively.

RUBBER DUCK DEBUGGING

A seemingly silly, but surprisingly effective way of debugging is something that is known as 'rubber duck debugging', or simply 'rubber-ducking'. This involves purchasing a rubber duck (like you might have in your bathtub) and perching it on your desk near your computer. You then explain in great detail to the duck (who knows nothing of programming or coding – it is just a duck) how things are supposed to be working in your code.

The theory is that coders will often realise the error of their coding when explaining how the code is *supposed* to work to a layperson (non-coder). This forces the coder to have to explain very specifically how the code is supposed to work, prompting an 'Aha!' moment when he suddenly realises the error, having discovered it himself. The duck just sits there, glad to have been of service and sworn to secrecy.

Just as you can see functions, variables, loops and algorithms in everyday life, you are actively debugging all the time. Any time you try to learn a new skill, you will make mistakes, but with practice and determination you will get better and better.

Big tech companies often have 'Bug Bounty' schemes, where users test programs to find bugs in their software for cash rewards.

TAKING IT FURTHER

Where Do You Go From Here?

As you start to consider creating more and consuming less code-related material, here are some pointers to help you along the way.

WHICH TOOL TO USE?

It is often said that the best tool you can use is the one that is currently in front of you. That might be a pen and paper, it might be your smartphone or your computer. Whatever tools you use, make sure that you get to know them well. Be ready and willing to help others with their toolkits too. Get to know your IDE inside and out (see page 58).

LEARN KEYBOARD SHORTCUTS

Not just for the sake of coding, but also to make yourself more efficient when using a computer. Every operating system and every program on a computer has a range of keyboard shortcuts to help you keep your hands from moving to the mouse or trackpad.

REQUIREMENTS AND FEATURES

When you get started, begin by writing out a base specification of the game or program that you want to make. Figure out the finer details later, because chances are that you'll never want to release your project into the wild until you think that it's 'perfect'. Set yourself a deadline so that you get used to releasing on time. What are your features? What are your limitations?

You may be tempted to put all of your ideas into one project. But be aware that if you do that, you may never reach the end of that project. It's good to be constrained by time and features to ensure that you actually ship. Plus all those ideas of yours can possibly become other projects in the future (just look at how many Angry Birds games there are!).

KEEP A JOURNAL

Sometimes the best technology you can keep next to you is a simple pencil and paper to note what you're doing, issues you need to fix and other things. Journalling is a really good way of measuring progress, plus if you journal with a pen/pencil and paper, it's a good way to take a break from the computer screen.

If you're a keen coder, your journal may soon become an integral part of your curriculum vitae. You never know how successful one of your projects might be!

STEP AWAY FROM THE DEVICES

Gone are the days of the typical computer nerd, hunched at his desk and gorging on junk food. You are the coders of the future, and you'll need to keep your brains fighting fit! Eat healthily, exercise, take regular breaks away from your devices and make sure you get enough sleep at night.

KEEP THE END USER IN MIND

That is, consider how the person using your program might think about it and use it. Remember that even if you are a coder, your ideal end user may not be – so you have to Think Like a User too! Make plans to test your code with other people so that you can get good feedback. End users and testers are the ones who might click or tap where you didn't intend them to, thus revealing a flaw in your programming. Remember that they are there to help you!

DON'T CODE ALONE

Don't code in a vacuum – try to find like-minded people to test your projects, who can provide insight and help along the way. Join coding communities online or local hackspaces to see how you can participate.

EMBRACE YOUR MISTAKES AND LEARN FROM THEM

Understand that things may not work right the first time. Embrace your mistakes and use them to make you stronger. Learn how to take constructive criticism (but also how to defend your decisions). As Einstein said, 'Failure in success is progress'.

COMMENT, COMMENT, COMMENT

Comment your code. You may think that you won't need to, but it's really important to keep your future self in mind for when you would like to revisit a project, or even if you collaborate with someone else. Commenting your code makes it easier and faster for you to get up and running on coding projects. Be descriptive when you comment, keeping in mind that the person may not understand the code at first and needs a guiding hand.

Make sure that when you make changes to your code, you also make changes to your comments accordingly!

BE A LIFELONG LEARNER

Never stop learning and don't be intimidated by the changing landscape of technology. It doesn't matter what age you are, you can always play an important part. Try to learn at least two programming languages. There will always be more to learn with coding, so embrace your love of learning and help others on their journey to think like a coder!

LEARN THE LANGUAGES OF OTHERS

As you learn how to code, remember that you will often have to communicate with non-coders on a regular basis. These may be your superiors, your clients, your co-workers and/or your loved ones. Getting an idea of the lens through which they view the world will help you become a better communicator, not just with computers, but with everyone else too!

LEND A HELPING HAND

Help other people get better. Volunteer to help others code. Study other code. Ask questions! The community is vast, waiting for you to become a part of it. What can you do to help make the world a better place for you and future generations?

TAKE TIME TO PLAN

Don't get ahead of yourself. Take the time to plan things out. Even if you have the most astonishingly awesome idea while you're in the middle of coding something else, just take the time to write it down and save it for later.

BACK UP YOUR WORK

Make sure that you save your work, and have a backup system in place – these days it's hard not to have some kind of backup system already in place on your computer. Learn how version control and committing your code changes to a repository work.

NEVER FORGET TO HAVE FUN

While it might be easy to get swept up into the more data- and business-orientated side of coding later in your career, don't forget that knowing how to code gives you one of the most awesomely creative means of self-expression. Take time to make a game, or an art visualisation or something for your family or community.

Coding for Change

WITH GREAT POWER . . .

One of the very first digital general-purpose computers in the 1940s, the ENIAC, was designed to help save lives. Although computers are used more for entertainment and content consumption these days, we have an opportunity now more than ever to leverage computing power and thinking like a coder to continue the trend of helping people.

A number of social movements have risen up in recent years from universities, companies and coding clubs around the world. They have one thing in common, and that is lending their expertise as coders to help effect positive change around the world. Whether it's helping design a website for a charity that sends spectacles to the disadvantaged in developing countries, or creating a noticeboard for volunteers at a medical-training company in South America, you can make a difference.

. . . COMES GREAT RESPONSIBILITY!

Thinking like a coder is now your superpower, and you get to choose how to use it – and it doesn't have to be a global initiative. It might be something as simple as volunteering at a local coding club, or helping teach someone three times your age to get a start coding at the same time as you. Ask around to see how you can help others on their journey as well as your own. Learning together is better, after all!

The ENIAC was actually programmed entirely by women, some of whom never gained recognition for their contributions within their lifetimes.

Time For One More Game?

UNICODE CIPHER WHEEL

If computers can count using binary to represent other numbers besides 0 and 1, then how do they understand anything else? Any number, symbol or letter is called a character, and computers can understand them as well. And binary isn't the only encoding system that computers use.

Opposite is an example of how the English language is displayed in a system called Unicode – and that's just the lowercase letters! There are different numbers for uppercase letters, punctuation and even other symbols. Thankfully, computer coding has moved on far enough that we don't need to know all of the Unicode characters. These days when we code we can do it using words.

Letter (lowercase)	Unicode value
a	97
b	98
c	99
d	100
e	101
f	102
g	103
h	104
i	105
j	106
k	107
l	108
m	109
n	110
o	111
p	112
q	113
r	114
s	115
t	116
u	117
v	118
w	119
x	120
y	121
z	122

Caesar Cipher

Over 2,000 years ago, Julius Caesar famously ciphered his important military messages (a cipher is when a letter is replaced by another letter or symbol) by shifting the letters three places along. A common way to represent this is with a cipher wheel. A cipher wheel consists of one wheel within another. The outer wheel displays the 26 letters of the alphabet. The inner wheel also displays the alphabet and rotates within the outer wheel.

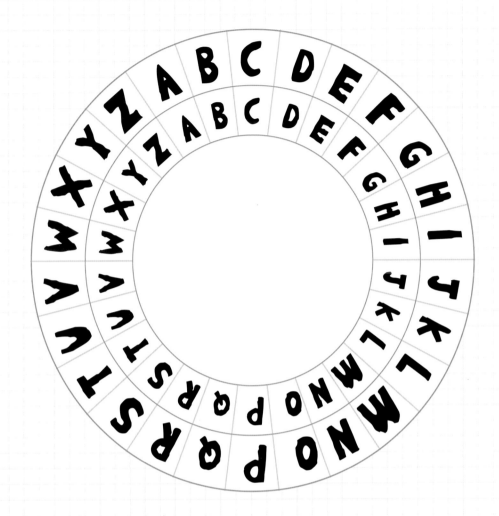

Build your own cipher wheel

Follow the instructions below to build your own cipher wheel and begin sharing secret codes with your friends.

    Photocopy (don't cut it out of the book!) the cipher wheel as you see it above. You will need one outer wheel and one inner wheel, so make two copies. Cut out both wheels (circles) and join them together in the centre with a paper fastener so they can both rotate. You could do the same using Unicode values on one ring.

Life, Thinking Like a Coder and Everything

Congratulations! You now know how to think like a coder, without even trying! So what does that even mean? Thinking like a coder means being able to solve problems and express yourself creatively. And chances are that you already know and do both of these things already.

The problem is that you probably haven't been shown how to look at all the aspects of your life through the lens of a coder yet!

- If you like to make music, you know how to think like a coder.
- If you like to come up with dance moves, you know how to think like a coder.
- If you like to play football, you know how to think like a coder.

Thinking like a coder, computational thinking, computer science – no matter how you hear the term, it isn't all about numbers and symbols or even code – it all comes down to creative problem-solving.

As we have seen, you don't even need to use a computer to do creative problem-solving. A computer is just another tool for you to use (alongside your rubber duck).

Thinking like a coder encompasses skill sets from reasoning, logic and mathematics, but is actually a really expressive medium for making things – awesome things. Computers aren't magic – they're completely under your control and you owe it to yourself to learn how they work. The mind of the creative problem-solver is much smarter and stronger than any computer in the world!

SAVE THE PACIFIC NORTHWEST TREE OCTOPUS

We've mentioned critical thinking before, and it's worth looking at it in more detail to explain exactly what is meant. We are, all of us, connected. With over 1 billion webpages as of 2014 and the amount of smartphone users expected to be 2.5 billion by 2019, there is little information that we cannot have access to in a very short amount of time. That doesn't necessarily mean that all information is accurate, however. Enter the Pacific Northwest Tree Octopus.

If you do a little research, you'll learn that the Pacific Northwest Tree Octopus is an endangered species normally found in the temperate rainforests of the Olympic Peninsula on the West Coast of North America. There is an extensive website detailing the plight of the tree octopus and how pollution and natural predators have forced it near the brink of extinction. You can sign up to a mailing list, hashtag your support on Twitter, or even buy a T-shirt and a coffee mug.

And yet the tree octopus does not exist. The website is a well-established internet hoax (since 1998!) that is now used to test internet literacy in schools. To this day, it continues to fool younger students into believing that the tree octopus is real and in danger of being eaten by a sasquatch.

Now it might seem obvious to some that an octopus living in the trees is just plain absurd, but when we have all the world's information at our fingertips (true and false), it can be difficult to identify the real from the fake.

The internet is one of the primary resource tools of the coder, and myriad solutions for coding problems are available from numerous websites. But before you begin searching for a quick fix to your problem, make certain that you understand your issue completely. Take the time to study the documentation for your programming language of choice and even try contacting a peer or mentor who knows about coding to help you out one-on-one. Analyse the answers you have been given and also evaluate where the solutions are coming from.

More on Computational Thinking

Computational thinking is broken down into four parts:

- Decomposition
- Pattern Recognition
- Abstraction
- Algorithm Design

All of these words sound very important, so let's break them down into simpler terms that we can understand better.

DECOMPOSITION

Think about how a movie is made and put together. The average Hollywood movie has a crew numbering in the thousands, from the visual-effects teams and the costumers, to the catering etc. Even though you may only see a limited number of actors on the screen at one time, and perhaps only know the name of the directors and producers, a huge team effort was made to ensure that the film was created and released. If we picture a Hollywood motion picture as a huge problem, then the cast and crew are the smaller pieces of the puzzle, all working together to solve it.

PATTERN RECOGNITION

Recognising patterns helps us solve problems where patterns exist, so this second step in computational thinking helps us to break problems down even further. For instance, you may at one point have had to recognise patterns before submitting information on a website. This kind of pattern recognition, known as a CAPTCHA, is in use by many online companies to prevent computers or automated software from 'pretending' to be human. Forcing the user to complete a pattern matching test accurately is our (current) working defence against such software.

In the CAPTCHA above, we have to identify all the pictures that contain trees. This isn't something a computer can do. Yet.

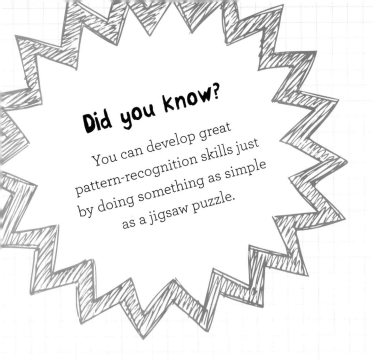

Did you know?

You can develop great pattern-recognition skills just by doing something as simple as a jigsaw puzzle.

ABSTRACTION

Let's say that I need to be at my friend Adam's house by 3:00pm on Saturday. I live 7.2 miles away from him. On Saturday morning, I'm feeding my lemur and going swimming. Then I'm going to a café north of town for 1:00pm to have lunch and should be done by 2:00pm. The café is 3.1 miles away from him. How much distance do I have to cover between 2:00pm and 3:00pm?

When we use abstraction, we take any non-relevant information away from the problem at hand. For instance, it doesn't matter how far away I live from Adam, because on Saturday afternoon I'll be closer to him. It also doesn't matter that I'm feeding my lemur or going swimming. The only pertinent information from the word problem is the distance between the café and Adam's house:

3.1 miles

I could probably walk it!

If we go back to looking at Hollywood blockbusters, think about a time when you watched a movie and were scared of something that you hadn't actually seen on the screen. Directors can potentially get around spending millions of dollars on special effects by filming shots of actors reacting to the monster 'off screen' instead and building up tension in the film!

ALGORITHM DESIGN

The last step of computational thinking involves coming up with a sequence of steps (an algorithm) to design and test against the problem you've distilled from decomposition, pattern recognition and abstraction. However, to explain it better, let's meet Johann Carl Friedrich Gauss.

Meet Gauss

If you were asked to add up all the numbers from 1 to 100 in your head, do you think you could do it? If so, how long might it take you?

The same task was given to Johann Carl Friedrich Gauss when he was eight years old, a long time back in the year 1785 (six years before Charles Babbage was even born). As the story goes, Gauss's teacher, hoping to occupy the class for a long period of time, assigned them the job of adding up all the numbers. Gauss quickly came up with the answer: 5,050.

Gauss didn't manually add up each individual number (1 + 2 + 3 . . . + 98 + 99 + 100). Instead, he noticed that there was a pattern in the numbers. If he added numbers together from either end of the set, they would equal the same thing: 1 + 100 = 101; 2 + 99 = 101; 3 + 98 = 101 and so on. There would only be a possible 50 pairs of numbers to add (50 being the halfway point between 1 and 100) so Gauss only had to multiply 50 x 101 to get the correct answer: 5050.

The Gauss Trick

Add up all numbers from 1–100

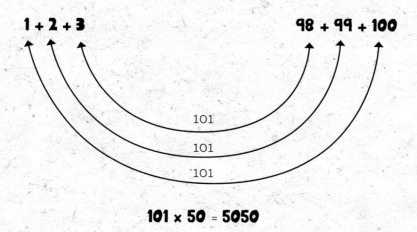

1 + 2 + 3   **98 + 99 + 100**

101

101

101

101 x 50 = 5050

Did you know?

Don't feel bad if you didn't spot the pattern that Gauss saw. He was a mathematical genius who made many important discoveries. When he died, he was buried without his brain – this was sent to Göttingen University, and it's still there now!

Gauss wasn't a computer scientist – there were no computers in his era – but he was a very clever kid. Gauss, at eight years old, was a creative problem-solver. He took a larger problem and decomposed it (broke it down into more manageable steps), then identified patterns (the addition of pairs on either end of the number set equalling the same). Through abstraction he removed any unnecessary steps – in this case, addition was no longer required to solve the problem, multiplication was.

It was once said by the notable science-fiction author and futurist Arthur C. Clarke that 'any sufficiently advanced form of technology is indistinguishable from magic'. The problem with magic is, that when it goes away, nobody knows how to bring it back! If we all learn how to think like coders, we can still hold on to the reins of technology as it gallops towards the future.

So what does a computer scientist or computational thinker actually look like? Look in a mirror and you'll soon find out!

Glossary

Algorithm A series of planned-out steps or rules that solves a problem (see page 70).

Artificial intelligence The ability for a computer to appear as intelligent as a human being.

Binary A system of numbers and counting relating to only two states: on and off (see page 20).

Boolean A date type with only two values: true or false.

Code Words or symbols that can be used to represent other words and symbols.

Comments Notes added to code to help yo9u to navigate it in the future (see page 117)

Condition The state of evaluating to true or false.

Constraints Limitations or constrictions that define the scope of a problem or project.

Core The part of the microprocessor that receives instructions and carries out actions and calculations based on those instructions.

Cross-platform Software or an app that is available on different systems (or platforms) and behaves the same. For example, the popular game Angry Birds is available on multiple computing and gaming platforms: iOS, Android, Windows Phone, Windows, MacOS, Playstation, XBox etc.

Data Pieces of information.

Data languages Languages that process data, such as 'R' for statistics, or SQL for working with databases.

Debugging The process of finding an error in your code that prevents it from working correctly (see page 107).

Denary A term that describes numbers we are used to using (i.e. 1–10), also known as decimal.

Efficient The process of achieving the maximum effect with the minimum amount of effort.

Encoding/Decoding The process of changing data into another format.

Evaluate To compare one value against another.

Executable A computer file, or program, that can be run. Computer programs are also sometimes referred to as 'executables'.

Execute The process of carrying out instructions given by a computer program.

File An object a computer uses to store data/information.

Flow diagram A visual representation of a process, with a start, end and steps in between (see pages 50–51).

IDE (Integrated Development Environment) A software tool that helps you write code.

Indented/Indentation Formatting your code with whitespace. Some programming languages require that there is the correct amount of space before each statement to ensure that the code is more easily read and executed.

Input/Output Information that goes into, and subsequently comes out of, a computer.

Internet of Things The increasing rise of internet-connected or 'smart' devices that can be interacted with from other devices or the internet. Categories may include light bulbs, toasters, thermostats etc.

Logic Principles of reasoning utilized to help you find solutions to coding requirements.

Logic bugs Errors in how instructions are carried out.

Loop An efficient method of repeating steps in a program without having to re-code them (see pages 73–87). Two types of loops are 'for loops' and 'while loops' (see page 75).

Further Reading

The history of coding and computing continues with your own journey. There are great resources to be found below.

CRITICAL THINKING AND LOGICAL REASONING

Almossawi, Ali, *An Illustrated Book of Bad Arguments* (Scribe UK, 2014). This book is free to read online at www.almossawi.com/bookofbadarguments.html.

Almossawi, Ali, *Bad Choices* (John Murray, 2017)

Carroll, Lewis, *The Complete Works of Lewis Carroll* (Penguin, 1998). A good introduction to a prolific writer. Further information can be found online at www.lewiscarroll.org/carroll/texts.

Gardner, Martin, *The Night is Large: Collected Essays, 1938-95* (Penguin, 1997). An introduction to the work of Martin Gardener, although the full breadth of his work can be found at www.martin-gardner.org.

MORE PEOPLE WHO HAVE SHAPED TECHNOLOGY

Bill Gates: https://en.wikipedia.org/wiki/Bill_Gates

Steve Jobs: https://en.wikipedia.org/wiki/Steve_Jobs

Linux Torvalds: https://en.wikipedia.org/wiki/Linus_Torvalds

Markus Persson: https://en.wikipedia.org/wiki/Markus_Persson

ORGANISATIONS WHO HAVE SHAPED TECHNOLOGY

The Electronic Frontier Foundation: https://www.eff.org/
The Raspberry Pi Foundation: https://www.raspberrypi.org/
Arduino: https://www.arduino.cc/en/Guide/Introduction
Open Source Initiative: https://opensource.org/

ONLINE LEARNING

Khan Academy: A free-to-use source for learning maths, science, coding and more at
   your own pace can be found at https://www.khanacademy.org/
Automate the Boring Stuff with Python: Al Sweigart's guide to practical programming
   can be found at http://automatetheboringstuff.com/
MIT's Scratch: https://scratch.mit.edu/
More resources available from coder.jimchristian.net

Index